If you have ever considered buying or selling a business, *... Don't Know What You Don't Know: A Step-by-Step Guide For Getting the Most From The Sale Of Your Business* is a turnkey, simple, easy-to-read and comprehend handbook for success.

Think of the book as the Swiss Army Knife for buying or selling a business. Every entrepreneur should think about and consider adding this book to their professional library. You will be able to decide what resources, if any, to deploy as you develop your game plan, since you will see the unique perspective from the buyer and the seller points of view.

Based on Steven Denny's own first-hand insightful knowledge and experience, he has personally guided hundreds of people just like you to achieve their life-long dreams. Steven's style is straightforward as he provides a proven path with a built-in GPS system.

Don't miss out! This could be one of the best investments that you could ever make.

BILL PRENATT
Co-owner
Simply Successful, LLC

Steven Denny has delivered a powerful and enlightening book that should serve as an invaluable roadmap for sellers wanting to maximize the value of their business. The sage advice is presented in a reader-friendly format that demystifies the selling process and will produce larger and quicker offers.

TIMOTHY C. NASH
President/CEO
American Bank of Missouri

Steve has done an excellent job of leading owners through the emotional, financial, and legal maze of selling one's business. It is comprehensive and his case study and illustrative characters make it fun and very easy to follow. This is a must-read for any business owner who wishes to achieve his definition of financial independence.

NED A MINOR
Attorney, Author
Deciding To Sell Your Business The Key To Wealth And Freedom

Steven Denny has hit the spot with this book. A must-read for business owners considering the sale of their business. Practical advice on the right approach to achieve your desired outcome. I highly endorse it.

GREG KELLS
M&AMI, LCBI, CMEA, CSBA, CBTS, BCA, Business Broker

Here's what I kept thinking while reading *You Don't Know What You Don't Know*: I wish I read this book before I sold my business last year. Steve knows what business owners go through when selling or buying a business. And he offers clear-eyed, practical, and valuable advice that can help any owner build their company and get maximum value when they're ready to sell.

TOM RUWITCH
Co-Owner and CEO of MarketVolt, LLC
(before selling the company in 2019)

In this book, Steve Denny has done an excellent job of explaining to business owners the importance of including an exit plan as part of their business plan. This is an important message for all business owners.

DICK MUELLER
CEO, Franchise Advisor
FranSelect

Maybe "*You Don't Know What You Don't Know*" when it comes to selling your business, but I can assure you Steve Denny does! My family has worked in the business brokerage industry for four generations. Having met and trained thousands of business brokers over the years, I can tell you Steve Denny is in an elite class. I would trust Steve to value and sell my own business any day.

RON WEST
President
Business Brokerage Press, Inc.

This book is a true gem for all those in the process of selling their business. *You Don't Know What You Don't Know: A Step-by-Step Guide for Getting the Most from the Sale of Your Business* is filled with the exact insight and instruction needed to enter into and close a successful sales transaction. I've worked closely with Steven Denny for over a decade and have witnessed first-hand his unmatched mergers and acquisition acumen, and keen sales mindset. Readers will be equipped with the MUST-HAVE knowledge and proven strategies to transition their business with ease.

ELIZABETH LEDOUX
CEO/Lead Strategist
The Transition Strategists

Every chapter of this book represents a mistake, an unrealistic expectation, or a blind spot of an otherwise enthusiastic and hardworking business owner that I have encountered or seen in my forty years of representing business owners in every stage of their businesses. This book is specific, concrete and practical guidance that will temper your expectations, open your eyes to the real world, and recalibrate your compass on this, the most important leg of your journey as a business owner.

BILL HIGLEY
Attorney
Saint Louis, Missouri

YOU DON'T KNOW
WHAT
YOU DON'T KNOW™

YOU DON'T KNOW
WHAT
YOU DON'T KNOW™

A STEP-BY-STEP GUIDE FOR GETTING THE MOST FROM THE SALE OF YOUR BUSINESS

STEVEN DENNY

Stonebrook Publishing
Saint Louis, Missouri

A STONEBROOK PUBLISHING BOOK

Copyright ©2021 by Steven Denny

This book was guided in development and
edited by Nancy L. Erickson, The Book Professor®
TheBookProfessor.com

Library of Congress Control Number: 2020917875

Hardcover ISBN: 978-1-7358021-6-9
Paperback ISBN: 978-1-7358021-0-7
eBook ISBN: 978-1-7358021-9-0

www.stonebrookpublishing.net

PRINTED IN THE UNITED STATES OF AMERICA

10 9 8 7 6 5 4 3 2 1

DEDICATION

This book is dedicated to my lovely wife Debi
who joined me more than forty years ago
and built us a wonderful home and family.
You mean the world to me.

CONTENTS

PREFACE

If you are thinking about selling your company, I wrote this book for you. Selling your business is probably the largest single transaction you'll experience in your lifetime, so great care and consideration should be taken. There are two ways to approach this process:

1. Do it yourself

2. Involve a team of professionals

This book will show you the path for both approaches.

As a professional business advisor, I've seen many instances where an owner chose to sell their business on their own. Business owners usually take this approach when a willing buyer approaches them, and the seller doesn't want to spend the money to get professional help. They prefer to pocket the fees they would have paid to involve a professional. I've seen many of these transactions close, but there have been only a few instances where the seller actually received what they expected and deserved from the transaction.

Why?

Because sellers *don't know what they don't know.*

This book provides an experienced view of how the process really works. Ultimately, my goal is to enable you to receive the full value for your business at closing. This happens when you follow a proven path.

The value of your business is built over time. If you take a shortcut on your exit strategy, you can leave a lot of money on the table. Investing the time and effort to follow a proven path dramatically increases your chances of a successful return. When properly executed, selling your business can be a life-changing event whereby you receive the full value for your career investment.

I strongly advocate for investing in the professional approach, but if you want to go the DIY route, this book can also help.

ARE YOU READY TO SELL?

"Why is this business for sale?"

Buyers ask this question to learn the seller's motivation and level of urgency. As the seller, you should answer this question in a way that doesn't lead a buyer to believe that you must sell, which can make buyers believe they have the most leverage in the transaction.

Remember that you have two things in common with buyers:

1. You both seek a good business fit.

2. You both seek a good value.

And that's where the similarities end. Buyers and sellers are quite different.

To be a good business fit, the buyer needs to see that they can successfully manage the business. Especially with an outsider, the buyer is not going to be emotionally connected to the history and legacy of your business; instead, they're solely focused on whether or not they can successfully operate it independently of the seller.

Buyers take a close look at the capabilities of a business and its employees to determine if they can step right in and assume control or if they'll need to make significant

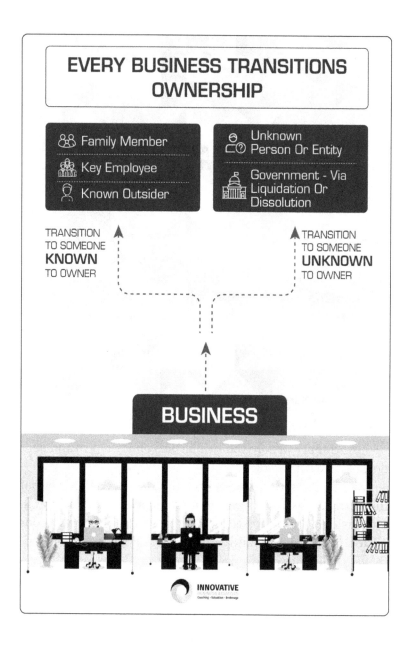

changes to get the business operating as they desire. If a buyer thinks a lot of change will be necessary, they know those changes will likely be costly, and they'll pay less for such a business.

Sellers typically evaluate the fit in a different way. They assess whether the buyer will be a good cultural fit for their business and wonder if they'll gel with current employees and customers. Sellers focus on legacy and often make judgments about whether or not the buyer will be a good steward of the business they've built.

To be a good value, the buyer must also see that the business provides an economic return commensurate with the current market, lending standards, and their own expectations. Since buyers are engaged in the market and are always looking for and evaluating potential opportunities, they're generally well-informed about current market values. They'll often have an entire team help them measure the value of an opportunity. This team can include a banker, appraiser, accountant, and maybe even a broker. Buyers are thorough and knowledgeable, and they often know the full range of value for the businesses they target.

The seller also wants a good value. The financial terms must be within their expectations. Unfortunately, it's quite common that the seller, unlike the buyer, doesn't have a well-informed understanding of the value of their business, especially in relation to the current state of the market. Quite often sellers go to market without a current valuation, without the counsel of professionals and without knowing what the current state of the transaction marketplace is. Thus, sellers are often at a disadvantage. But sellers do know what they're willing to sell for, so if they get acceptable terms, they often still feel they've received good value.

Because it's common for buyers to be at an advantage when it comes to evaluating the economic value of a business, sellers need to be able to answer the following three questions:

1. What will you do the day after
the deal closes?

You'll be much better off if you have a plan for your life after the sale. It could be that the business has defined your life, and, in some ways, it was your life. After the sale, you'll have to retrain your mind and body to break the long-established habit of going to work. It can be a difficult emotional trial, but if you come up with a new life objective before the sale, you'll have a much easier time transitioning after the close.

If you think of nothing more than sleeping in and playing a round of golf, you're fooling yourself. Without a goal or plan, you'll get bored and life will be unfulfilling. It's a recipe for unhappiness, and you may even regret selling your business. You need a new purpose. If you don't have a plan for after the sale, then you may not be ready to sell. Before you sell your business, figure out what you'll do in the days, months, and years ahead.

You might have a chance to be engaged in your business after the sale. The buyer may ask you to stay on for a specific period of time to ensure customer retention, to perform various consulting functions, or to help with other responsibilities in the transaction. In such cases, the purchase agreement will include a consulting agreement or employment contract that clarifies your duties.

This kind of involvement after the sale can make the transition easier. It gives you time to express appreciation to your former customers and employees without the responsibility of ownership. Even though you may disagree with the decisions the buyer makes, your tenure is coming to an end and you can look forward to the next chapter in your life.

It's not unusual for the buyer to say they're capable of running the business alone before the end of your specified term. Then you can exit early, feeling satisfied that you helped the buyer learn as much as they wanted to learn about the business operations. You can leave with a clear conscience and a sense of closure.

2. Why is the business for sale?

Again, this is often the first question a buyer asks. Your answer should support or enhance the value of the sale.

Positive Answers:

- I want to retire and enjoy the fruits of my labor.
- There's a new business opportunity for me.
- The business has grown beyond my capabilities.
- It's part of my strategic plan.

These are reasonable answers. They show that you're leaving the business for personal reasons, not because the business is failing. Don't answer in a way that rouses the buyer's suspicions. For example, if a thirty-five-year-old says they're selling so they can retire, the buyer might raise an eyebrow and dig a little deeper.

Here are some answers that might be red flags to the buyer:

- The business is in trouble, and I don't know what to do.
- I'm having issues with employees and/or customers.
- The business is changing, and I don't want to change with it.
- A competitor is infringing on our business.
- A family member has a health problem.
- There are regulatory issues.

These answers convey a sense of foreboding, desperation, and/or urgency. The buyer will worry that the business is in trouble. They'll also realize that time is more important to you than money, and a savvy buyer will use that knowledge to their advantage. They'll place a discounted value on your business, which may result in an offer that is less than you desire.

When the buyer asks why you're selling, your positive answer will set the tone and play an important role in establishing the economic value of the company.

3. Am I prepared for this to be personal?

You probably think of your business in personal terms and even use personal pronouns and phrases like *my business*. Selling it will be an emotional and personal decision.

It's not that way for buyers.

Buyers think of a business by the business name, like Smith Hardware or Main Street Grocery. They'll purchase a company for the business entity itself, not for the personal pride of ownership.

These are two highly contrasting emotional spaces. You're thinking personal; they're thinking impersonal. Thus, the emotional premium is absent for the buyer. They don't remember what it was like when the business was first starting out, and they have no attachment to the sacrifices you made to build it. They don't know that your children worked there after school and that when you invested in lighting fixtures, it was at the expense of your family vacation.

Buyers don't have that emotional attachment.

Rest assured that your emotional attachment will come into play during the price negotiations. The buyer will offer a price that's significantly lower than what you want or deserve. You'll be offended, may refuse to participate, and could lose the sale entirely. Of course, you're the one who actually loses the most in such a situation. If you aren't prepared to put your emotions aside or aren't capable of doing so, then you might not be ready to sell your business.

Let's see this in action. Bill and Mark are two very different sellers with two very different business sale experiences. We'll follow their stories throughout this book.

BILL AND MARK

The time to sell came quickly for Bill when the business cash flow deteriorated. Every day, he hoped for a miraculous infusion of cash to restore profitability. But costs kept growing while revenues fell. Bill treated his employees like family, so he refused to reduce their hours or lay anyone off. To fill the cash hole, he borrowed from family members and his savings, hoping he wouldn't have to ask for more.

Finally, the situation became untenable. His mentor convinced him there was only so much cash left, and at his current run rate, he'd run out of cash within a matter of months and would be forced to close.

Bill tried to sell the business on his own. He was well known within his community and, confidentially, he began to tell his peers and bankers that he wanted to sell. He expected them to help him and recommend someone as a potential buyer; instead, he was shocked by their reaction.

His banker became more interested than ever in the performance of the business. He kept very close tabs on Bill's account balances and phoned to check on him as his payment dates approached. Bill was initially flattered by the attention, but he slowly came to realize the bank was alarmed and wanted to make sure they'd get paid. The bank requested additional information from him, and the tones of their conversations turned somber.

Meanwhile, Bill still had no credible buyer leads, so he decided to approach his largest vendor. That was a bad decision. The vendor became worried about his ability to get paid and changed his billing terms to a cash on delivery payment basis, which further restricted Bill's already strained cash flow. In the past, the vendor had always stressed "partnership" and "support of product," but when Bill asked them to issue credit and return some of the slow-moving merchandise, they wouldn't accommodate his request.

Eventually, Bill spoke with a few people who seemed interested in buying the business, but when he talked about the pressures he was facing, he scared them off. He wasn't truly prepared to sell and, therefore, couldn't give a positive answer to the question: "Why is your business for sale?"

Mark had a much different experience. He'd built his company over several decades and was now beyond normal retirement age. He'd been a good student of successful business practices and had implemented many of them. His business, although small, provided a low six-figure income for his family. The business had its inevitable ups and downs, but Mark had taken the time to think through a succession plan and had invested in trusted advisors to help him structure it properly. His path to retirement looked clear.

And then the plan changed. A buyer approached Mark, and for the first time, he considered selling his business to an outsider. Before going too far, Mark went back to his trusted advisors and consulted them on the proper approach to take.

All his advisors recommended that he hire an expert in the field to help with the sale—a business broker to assist with the process. After much review and investigation, he engaged the services of a seasoned broker who had years of experience representing companies of comparable sizes to his. Mark took the emotion out of the selling process and relied on professional guidance to reach his goals.

He learned that his reason for selling actually supported the value he was bringing to the marketplace. He used his reason for selling—that he wanted to retire— as an incentive to potential buyers. He was prepared to offer them ongoing consultation at no additional cost. The fact that they could have a seasoned veteran by their side as the business transitioned to a new owner was a benefit. In the end, working with a broker taught Mark to stress the positive elements of his business and to provide a plan of action to address any weaker elements of his value proposition.

Because Mark had learned so much from his broker—the value of his business, the current market conditions, and the specific elements of value his business represented—it made his interactions with potential buyers exciting. His enthusiasm was infectious, and buyers responded accordingly.

HOW DO YOU START?

Because he continued to hope that his DIY approach was the best use of his time and money, Bill spent months talking with his peers, bankers, and suppliers, and all he had to show for his efforts was increased pressure and frustration. There were no buyer prospects on the horizon, and his account balances were shrinking. He was increasingly desperate, and the more he shared his plight, the more he repelled people.

Mark, however, was busy. With the help of an expert, he went through a comprehensive valuation process and clearly understood where his business was strong and where it was weak. His broker educated him about the market, and Mark learned about businesses similar to his that were also for sale. He learned about the various types of buyers, what was most important to them, and how to position his company for each buyer type. He was delighted to find out that he'd probably get more than he anticipated for the sale of his business. Just thirty days after he decided to consider an outside buyer, he began to connect with interested, qualified buyers.

The difference between Mark and Bill? Mark had a plan. Bill had a problem.

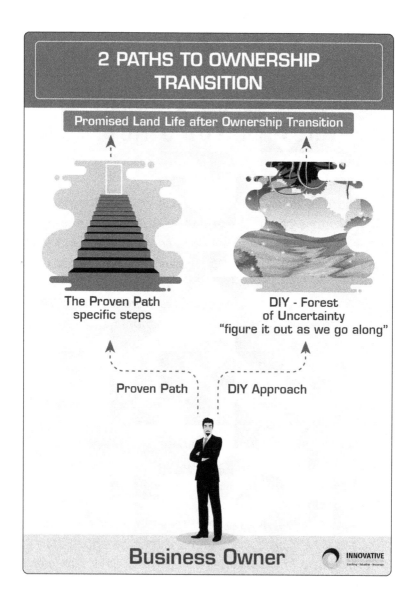

GET A PLAN

People can sell a business on their own if they're scrappy enough to take the knocks and learn from them and to pivot and move on to a more successful outcome. However, the DIY road is long and jagged and a difficult choice for most sellers.

The average business owner doesn't know how to sell a business. In fact, most only sell a business once or twice in their lifetime, so it makes sense to enlist an expert with extensive transactional experiences.

By vocation, brokers and advisors market businesses. Many specialize in specific industries, markets, or business sizes. Successful brokers follow a process and create a plan to generate good results. And it's comforting to know that they're wholly invested in your sale because that's how they make a living. No sale, no fee earned.

The process is similar for all brokers and advisors. In the simplest terms, they create documents which summarize the performance of your business, develop and enact a marketing plan, and engage with potential buyers. After the buyer commits to the purchase, brokers manage a due diligence process and help coordinate the closing and transfer of funds. The broker manages all aspects of the transaction and keeps all parties accountable for their responsibilities and timelines.

However, brokers and advisors don't do all this work alone. It's a team effort. They help a business owner assemble a team and get each team member focused on a specific role and outcome. Let's look at this in more detail.

ASSEMBLE A TEAM

A business is a complex organization with its own track record, customers, employees, and products and services. Extracting the highest value from a business sale requires a detailed game plan and experts in key positions. At a minimum, the sellers and buyers will each need to form a team which includes legal professionals, accounting and tax professionals and, potentially, lenders. It may also include human resource professionals, appraisals and valuation experts, and market experts. The team objective is to identify the significant aspects of the business that contribute to its value and apply professional expertise to access that value.

Extracting the highest value from a business sale requires a detailed game plan and experts in key positions.

The broker or advisor is responsible for creating a game plan with you. They'll identify areas where experts are required. Their objective is to use these experts in the most cost-effective manner. After all, the overall objective is for you to realize the highest and best value.

You may have an existing relationship with various experts and want to involve your existing bookkeeper and attorney during the process. But you should check with them to ensure that they have current and relevant experience helping owners transition their business. It's quite common to find that they don't have the expertise required to sell a business, and they may even feel somewhat overwhelmed by the process.

The most important factor to consider is the level of experience that's required from each professional. For example, selling a business requires very specific experience with certain aspects of business law. Your attorney may have helped you with various tasks like setting up your business structure, filing the required registrations, reviewing the property lease, and helping with various personal issues like trusts and traffic tickets. But when you're selling your business, the attorney you select should be experienced in negotiating and drafting definitive purchase agreements. Your best source for attorneys of this specialty is often your usual attorney who can recommend a specialist to you if this isn't their specialty. Highly specific terms will be negotiated and detailed in the various agreements that pertain to the transfer of business ownership, and you'll need a specialist attorney to get the best value from the transaction.

The same situation applies to the accountant. Most business accountants do an excellent job recording the financial activity of a business and producing the required financial reports. But few accountants have substantial experience with transaction work. A transaction often requires specific actions that have a direct effect on the tax liability of the seller.

Accountants with minimal transaction experience don't often have detailed knowledge about how specific terms and structures can impact a deal. And tax laws change regularly enough that seemingly unrelated legislation can have a substantial impact on a seller's net proceeds. For the best value results, sellers should engage accounting professionals who have current and thorough experience with mergers and acquisitions.

When you have a skilled attorney and accountant involved during the early stages of a sale, you and your broker or advisor can map out a plan for the best outcome. The professionals will determine the ideal *form* of the transaction, the ideal *timing* of the transaction, the ideal payout *terms* for the transaction, and the best way to *limit your risk and exposure* while conveying the business.

> *The professionals will determine the ideal form of the transaction, the ideal timing of the transaction, the ideal payout terms for the transaction, and the best way to limit your risk and exposure while conveying the business.*

Of course, you'll have to spend some money up front for these professionals; however, that might be the best money you'll ever spend because it can lead to lower costs later in the transaction and much higher net proceeds from the sale. In addition to a better return, involving these professionals from the beginning can expedite the transaction and reduce the level of stress, frustration, and unwelcome surprises throughout the process and after the closing.

When you've assembled the right team and the plan is developed, it's time to move on to the specifics, which involve at least three important steps:

Step 1 – Set the Target Price
Step 2 – Build the Marketing Documents
Step 3 – Put the Marketing Plan into Motion

Step 1: Set the Target Price

Setting your target price begins with a business valuation. A comprehensive business valuation examines all major elements of your business and identifies its strengths and weaknesses. A common misconception is that a business valuation only looks at the financials. In fact, a comprehensive valuation looks at the money, the people, the processes, the customers, the suppliers, the market, and the competitors. When you understand how the business is positioned in each of these areas, you can then determine its value.

It's important to differentiate a *comprehensive valuation* from a *financial valuation*. Typically, a financial valuation examines only the past financial performance of the business. It involves a series of calculations using financial data found in common business reports: cash flow statement, operating statement, balance sheet, and tax returns. A financial valuation provides a great amount of information but is limited by its focus on only one dimension of value—the financial dimension of the company.

In contrast, a comprehensive valuation process measures the financial dimension *plus* at least seven other pertinent

dimensions of value (more on this in Chapter 7). It measures the business against its industry, market, and competitors. It clearly details areas that enhance and reduce the value.

A comprehensive valuation helps you see the bare facts. It also helps take the emotion out of the equation and grounds your thinking in reality, which puts you in a much stronger position when the time comes to evaluate offers from buyers. You'll be able to see how your business compares to its peers. Sellers rarely compare themselves to their peers, but it can be a particularly gratifying practice when your business outperforms them in many areas. You'll discover a range of value for your business in its current position in the market. This range will set the parameters you and your broker or advisor will use to set the best target price in your market plan.

Step 2: Build the Informational Documents

Next, you'll need to assemble the marketing documents. These include documents like marketing flyers, information packets, confidential disclosure agreements, confidential information memorandums, and so on. These document packages can vary from business to business.

The objective of assembling these documents is to protect your interests as the seller, while also illustrating all the pertinent facts of the business to the buyer. The package should contain enough information so that a buyer can make an indication of interest or initial offer based on the information provided.

Buyers almost always want to see the business firsthand. This can be disruptive for many types of businesses, so thankfully virtual tours and pictorials can often address the demand. At its best, your document package will be comprehensive enough to enable buyers to make an initial offer sight unseen. It should also cover every aspect of the business. Invariably, buyers will ask for specifics. Some will be more interested in the personnel and their capabilities, while others will want to learn about any intellectual property included in the transaction.

A comprehensive document package demonstrates that you're prepared to execute on a transaction immediately. Buyers appreciate a quick response and will demonstrate their appreciation with quick offers.

> *A comprehensive document package demonstrates that you're prepared to execute on a transaction immediately.*

While the information documents are designed to provide a comprehensive overview of the business, they aren't inclusive of strategic facts or trade secrets that competitors could use. These are delicate issues and need to be handled with care. Competitors engaged in the discovery process will routinely ask for information, and advisors are experienced with keeping them engaged while protecting your interests.

There's yet another benefit of the informational documents that I never appreciated until my clients mentioned it to me. They've told me that these documents became treasured mementos of their business after its sale. The documents actually memorialize the businesses they have built, and allows them to point with pride to the economic value of their business and reflect on how the buyer ultimately received that or, in some cases, even a premium above the value asked.

Step 3: Put the Marketing Plan into Motion

Brokers market to three different types of buyers: lifestyle buyers, economic buyers, and strategic buyers. Each type of buyer has its own unique interests and will have different motivations. A successful marketing plan should be specifically tailored to address each type of buyer.

Lifestyle buyers want a business that they can work in.

They thrive on work that interests them and that compliments the lifestyle they wish to lead. They want to own and operate a business they personally identify with, and they usually want a business that's located in their own town or neighborhood. They strive for the freedom to set their own pace and to make a comfortable living serving their passion and its market. Lifestyle buyers typically want to learn all the same business details as the other buyer types, but their evaluation of the business is more heavily weighted to its location and alignment with their own passion.

Economic buyers see a business as a cash-generating machine. They focus on how a business performs, so they like to have a comprehensive set of financial documents to evaluate. They ultimately want to know how much cash a business produces. They prize stability and steady growth as it demonstrates a history that they expect to see continued. They also like to see minimal employee turnover and a large customer base with no single customer representing a significant portion of the revenue. They drill into financial valuations and will often lead with a discounted cash flow valuation methodology. Safety and consistency are highly important business traits for them.

Strategic buyers evaluate an opportunity based on the potential synergy with other businesses they already own or seek to acquire. They want a thorough understanding of all aspects of a business, and they'll factor out duplication and overlap to determine the combined value with their own company. Sometimes the primary synergy is a combination of products or services, or adding a new customer market, or hiring competence and capability. There are many ways that strategic buyers evaluate a business, but it's always in combination with an existing business or with another business they're seeking to acquire.

The marketing plan is designed to speak directly to each type of buyer. The information it contains highlights the benefits each type will receive from the potential purchase of the business.

YOU'RE READY TO SELL; IS YOUR BUSINESS READY?

Bill and Mark were both ready to sell, but their businesses were in vastly different places. Bill was incredibly anxious for a sale. He was under tremendous pressure, and he feared losing everything he'd spent his adult years building. His business was quickly running out of cash, and he'd soon be forced to close the doors because he wouldn't be able to pay his staff or his vendors. He imagined selling most of his family's possessions, including their home.

Even after that, he'd still be in trouble. He'd still be responsible for a huge business loan that he and his wife had personally guaranteed. With his continual worry, Bill never stopped to consider if the business was properly positioned to sell. He simply hoped he could hand over the keys and walk away.

Mark was now ready to entertain a sale. Like Bill, he'd founded and grown his business over several decades and was ready to step away. But Mark dreamed of finding a buyer who'd love his business like he did and would have the skills to take it to the next level. He hoped he could watch his business grow and prosper through the remainder of his life—much like the pride he experienced watching his children grow and prosper. To realize that dream, the business had to be positioned to give the new owner the highest probability of success.

Neither Mark nor Bill had any idea how to ensure their businesses were properly positioned. Mark asked himself what a buyer would want to know, and he quickly recognized that he didn't know how to answer that question. So, he went to his accountant and his attorney to get their input. Both advised him to seek an outside expert who specialized in that knowledge.

Bill never thought to ask that question. His accountant was aware of his distress, but Bill never asked for help, and the accountant never volunteered it. Bill did speak with his banker and asked for his help to temporarily lower his payment and help him find a buyer, but the banker was more concerned about Bill repaying him than with helping him.

How does a business position itself for ownership transfer? Here are three key characteristics that require your specific action to properly prepare a business for transfer.

THREE KEY CHARACTERISTICS
1. Current, complete, and accurate financial records

Read each word of this first pillar carefully. *Current* means that your financial statements are up-to-date to the prior month of the current year. *Complete* means that you also have a full set of historical operating financial documents and tax returns available. *Accurate* means that your documents are representative of the activities of the business and if they have been amended, include explanations.

These records will be used to calculate the financial aspects of the valuation and to illustrate the performance of the business over time for any prospective buyers. Buyers often request this set of documents first, so these documents form the critically important first impression.

Why do buyers want to see these documents first? Because buyers always want to know how much a business would earn for them if they owned it. These documents allow them to evaluate and determine how much they can invest to attain ownership and remain profitable.

Buyers always want to know how much a business would earn for them if they owned it.

Because your statements are current, it demonstrates that you are conscientious and understand that current data is necessary to successfully manage business performance. The business financial records are the key performance statistics and indicators of future performance. When the records are current, the potential buyer will have increased confidence.

If a buyer is going to use leverage or loans to help finance the purchase, then a complete set of financial documents are required for underwriting a loan. The lender will use these statements to prove that the business can adequately handle the debt. They do so by analyzing the timing and quality of the earnings and the total cashflow that the business has demonstrated the ability to deliver, so there's sufficient cash to cover the proposed debt and enough profit to enable the business to continue.

Complete sets of statements show all the pertinent information to potential buyers. Your tax returns illustrate how you've utilized current tax law to minimize tax obligations, while accurately reflecting business performance. The operating statements show the movement of cash through the business, detail all the operating costs, and illustrate how capital has been put to work in the business. It also validates the asset values.

Current and complete financial records provide buyers and financiers with the information necessary to perform a financial evaluation of the business. Providing a comprehensive set of documents will begin a potential transaction on a positive note.

2. Good business records

Business records are comprised of every agreement with every supplier, customer, and employee, along with all documented processes and procedures of a business. This can add up to an enormous amount of paper. *Good* business records are complete, current, and relevant.

It's important to note that a business may sometimes have verbal agreements. In such cases, you may need to convert these verbal agreements to written agreements, particularly if they deviate from your other records, so they can be easily conveyed to the buyer.

All of your contracts are included in this category. They should be complete and current, and they should also be easily transferrable to a new owner. Many times, contracts include specific language that deals with a change of control (such as a business owner selling) or transferability of the agreement. Agreements may even prohibit this type of activity or immediately terminate when this activity occurs. They could also trigger an automatic change of price or other term.

It's critical that you understand the terms of each contract and what impact any change of ownership may have on the business, so you can accurately convey this information to a potential buyer. This will be addressed further in subsequent chapters.

Patents, trademarks, copyrights, and other intellectual property are also included under this umbrella. Business owners seldom use these business records after issuance, but potential buyers commonly review these records. These records should be easily accessible and appropriately represented to potential buyers.

Your employee documents must also be in order and easily accessible. You may not want to disclose the particulars from these files during the marketing phase, but you'll have to share them during the due diligence period. All employee files should be accessible and complete with all required forms and signatures. Privacy laws are changing, so it's a good practice to review what can be shared and what must be retained by the seller early in the process.

> *Business records are any written records that are pertinent to the business. To be good business records, they should be easily accessible, complete, and current.*

Business records are any written records that are pertinent to the business. To be *good* business records, they should be easily accessible, complete, and current. A buyer will greatly appreciate comprehensive and readily available information.

3. Market price supported by the business performance

Every business has at least eight dimensions of enterprise value (the value of the business in dollars and cents). We'll discuss this in great detail in chapter 7, but for now, I want to stress that your business must meet a third major criterion in order to be marketed and it's this: the business performance must support the asking price in the current market.

> *The business performance must support the asking price in the current market.*

Market conditions change over time. Selling a business is no different than selling any other good or service. The present market has a major effect on the price. The marketability of a business is affected by the condition of the business *and* the condition of the current market. A strong business in a buyer's market will end up with a lower valuation than the same strong business in a seller's market.

Business performance also changes over time. However, it normally takes two to three years to effect a change that has a measurable impact on the business and price. Trends often matter more than change. Buyers seek businesses that have positively trended over an extended period of time. A growth trend signals that a business is resonating with its client base and delivering an ever-appreciating value to its market. A positive trend is a flashing *BUY NOW* sign because the price will likely increase if the buyer waits. A strong growth trend is highly sought after and will garner large interest and potential purchase activity from buyers.

On the other hand, negatively trending business performance is a flashing *WAIT* sign for buyers because a business exhibiting this trend will likely get cheaper over time. If buyers purchase now at a higher price, the probability of generating a return on invested capital is lower. This is the classic turnaround or fix and flip opportunity in business. Sellers in this position must recognize that there are very few buyers who are skilled enough to catch the proverbial falling knife and come away unharmed. The scarcity of buyers inherently makes the market condition more favorable to the few buyers looking to purchase, which leads to lowered price offerings.

The current market also has a significant impact. Are there businesses of a similar size and category also available on the market? Is access to capital via traditional channels such as bank financing readily available, or is it a tight market? Is the specific industry contracting or expanding? Are the industry trends positive or negative? Is the business located in a vibrant area with plenty of available market share, or is the business a dominant player in a shrinking market?

Many factors come into play regarding the current position of the market, and these factors must be accounted for when deciding the terms and price for a business. Engaging multiple buyers to compete simultaneously is the key the achieving the best sale price.

Mark had the right motivation to sell his business and was taking the time to learn about the sales process. He learned that he needed additional help beyond his accountant and attorney and how to find such necessary experts. The business was already doing well, but Mark knew that if he improved it further, it would give the next owner the strongest probability of success. Mark was on the right path.

A broker joined Mark's team, and Mark agreed to follow the process. The broker told him that his business financial records needed work. Thankfully, they were current. But they were formatted in a way that would be hard for an outsider to understand. The information was solid; the format was shaky.

Mark, with the counsel of his broker, embarked on a process to clean up the documents and transfer them into a traditional and easy-to-comprehend format. The team also put together a financial summary that tied the operating reports and tax returns together and clearly illustrated that the business was performing well over time. Trends were identified and pointed out, and Mark felt accomplished and able to justify his higher-than-average offering price.

Bill, on the other hand, was clueless. He needed to sell his business because it was distressed, and this really limited his options in ways he didn't appreciate.

He experienced slammed doors and discomfort as his banker and supplier turned up the pressure on him and his business.

The business conditions were less than desirable. The trends were all downward, and because they had a reduced inventory and a complete sell-out of some of their high-volume products, his customers began to realize that the business was unstable. With reduced sales, Bill cut back hours and staff count. Daily maintenance and sanitation practices suffered. The business was rapidly deteriorating.

Bill was so consumed with worry and new issues that he fell a few months behind on finalizing reports from his bookkeeper and accountant. The financial records began to slip. Like Mark, the format of the financial reports was cumbersome and not easily understood by an outsider. Bill was overwhelmed because so many areas needed his attention.

Like many businesses that had grown over several decades, the balance sheet had a number of entries that reflected the owner's lifestyle more than the business requirements, which clouded the view for a prospective buyer. The information was certainly accurate and lawful, but some line items were unclear and often not pertinent to the performance and health of the business. Bill had no idea his financial records looked opaque to an outsider.

The business records were in an even worse state. Bill had never considered that he might need to adjust terms and contracts in the event that he would want to sell his business, and there were even agreements that made a transfer difficult and made his business almost unsellable. Even if Bill could find a buyer and agree on an acceptable price, there were many vendors who wouldn't honor the current terms, which would change the business complexion and cost structure in such a way as to make the sale virtually unworkable.

However, there was one silver lining. The market was in Bill's favor. Changes were happening in his industry, and the geographic area favored his business. But Bill couldn't recognize these advantages because he didn't have the experience or expertise.

So, he continued to reduce his asking price. He hoped that if he lowered it enough someone would bite. But that's not what happened. His air of desperation scared buyers away. Price was not the problem—Bill was the problem.

CHAPTER
4

HOW LONG DOES IT TAKE TO SELL?

Bill was down but not out. He'd been speaking with his advisors, his lenders, his suppliers, and select members of his community for several months now. As his prospects narrowed, his desperation grew. He was running out of options and ideas.

Mark also learned he had some work to do. There were specific steps he had to take regarding inventory and assets to make the sale process happen the way he'd dreamed. He had the time to clean up and justify changes before the sale process began, which strengthened his position as a seller and made the business more attractive for a larger pool of buyers. Mark had been as diligent and detailed about the rest of his business records as he was over his financial documents, but it was still a large task to go through a methodical review and clean up areas that would impact the purchase transaction.

For example, Mark had a facility lease for his building. When he'd renewed the lease a few years prior, he'd already known the future term might be impacted by his succession plan. At that time, he'd requested and received a transfer clause in his renewal, but now after reviewing the document with his selling team, Mark discovered that the lease transfer would actually require the approval of the landlord and wouldn't release him from being personally liable for the lease. Mark hadn't foreseen this and had to take steps to make the outcome more in line with his expectation. But again, he'd created the time and space to do so before going to market.

Mark's advisor asked many questions and instructed him to pull together a vast amount of documentation. Mark already knew his business had grown steadily and was doing well, but now the analysis and trends pointed out strengths and weaknesses that encouraged Mark and made him feel even more proud of what he'd accomplished. Sure, he had many tasks to complete to prepare for the offering, but Mark was energized and excited about the path in front of him.

THE PATH

Whether you engage a professional team or attempt to sell your business on your own, the path is very similar. The steps may vary by industry and business entity type, but the path itself is the same. There are seven distinct steps:

1. Decision to Sell
2. Build a Team
3. Assessment
4. Informational Documents
5. Marketing
6. Diligence
7. Closing

Each step takes as long as necessary. Some steps happen very quickly, and some take much longer than expected because

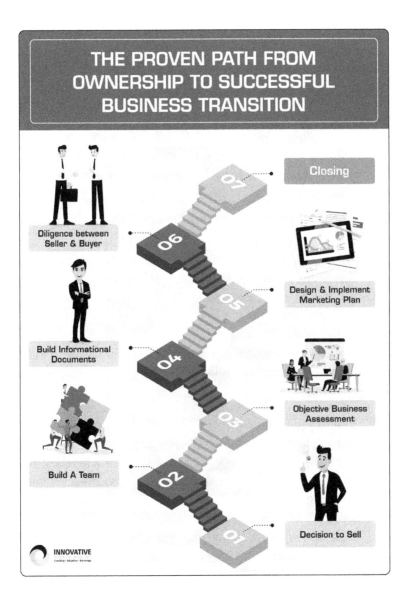

they involve outsiders whose time and priorities may not be aligned with yours. Whether or not you plan for them, all six steps will eventually be completed. The difference is that a DIY seller will often have to take two steps forward and one step back, whereas a seller who works with a team of experienced advisers can walk straight through the steps.

> *The difference is that a DIY seller will often have to take two steps forward and one step back, whereas a seller who works with a team of experienced advisor can walk straight through the steps.*

The buyer can also impact the amount of time each step takes. They might be anxious to close and want to expedite a process, or they might slow the process in hopes of negotiating a better purchase price. The buyer's motivation often establishes the timeline.

Let's look at these steps in detail and discuss how they each impact the process and timeline.

1. Decision to Sell

Deciding to sell is often the most difficult part of the journey for those owners who dreamed up, started, and built their own business. The business is an extension of who they are and defines what they do each day and who they interact with. Making the decision to sell is the most significant step on the path.

That decision means they also spend a lot of time thinking about who will be the perfect buyer. Owners often think of family, key employees, and competitors as they begin to go over the list in their mind. The legacy they leave is often forefront in their mind and selecting the "right" person to take the business into the future is a process they think about in detail. If the seller can't identify the right person, that's often an indication that they need help.

Once the decision is made, sellers often forget to think about what they'll do after the sale. It's quite common for sellers to spend a lot of time and effort arriving at the decision to sell, but very little time thinking about what personal impact the transition will have on them. This is what we call the "Day One Plan," and we strongly counsel sellers to have a well thought out long-range plan for what they will do on Day One of the rest of their life.

2. Build A Team

Even a DIY seller will eventually need a team to complete the sales transaction. They'll typically engage an outsider on a transactional basis to perhaps review a document or advise on various steps in the transition process. This transaction contractor's involvement and engagement are defined and restricted to commenting on a single element of the transaction, which may or may not be in concert with your overall objectives. Their opinion is only pertinent to that single transactional component.

Let's say you hire an attorney to provide an opinion on a document. He or she will comment on the lawfulness and accuracy of it. The transaction contractor won't advocate for a party's benefit or the structuring for a particular party's benefit. They won't know all the circumstances surrounding the transaction and won't be privy to the motivations and objectives of the parties. They'll have a very limited view of the transaction and will only comment on the particulars in front of them. Therefore, they might not be in sync with what you want to achieve.

This is entirely different from engaging an attorney as part of an assembled team at the start of the selling process. When an attorney is engaged from the beginning, they'll be able to advocate for their client's overall goal. They'll draft, review, and negotiate terms with that overall goal in mind.

Teams always protect the interest of the party they represent. They pay attention to the details and make sure they achieve the best possible outcome for their side of the transaction. Buyers often have an assembled team. If you choose to represent yourself as the seller, you might find that you're sitting alone, across the table from the buyer and their full team. The buyer's team will always want to control the deal timing and the document production because it gives them the best chance to get what they want out of the transaction. While they may consider your requests, their intent is to structure the transaction in a way that clearly benefits them as buyers. This puts the solo seller at a disadvantage and can lead to giving up terms and conditions that have significant impacts.

Sellers may choose the DIY approach because hiring a team costs money, and they want to spend as little as possible to net larger proceeds. But what actually happens is often the opposite. When the buyer has a team but a seller doesn't, the terms can be skewed toward the buyer and the seller can end up losing more money than if they'd hired a team.

> *Sellers may choose the DIY approach because hiring a team costs money, and they want to spend as little as possible to net larger proceeds. But what actually happens is often the opposite.*

For example, let's talk about an *earn-out*. That's when a buyer pays you for your business over time—after the ownership has changed—based on the actual performance of the business as compared to the targeted performance of the business. Statistically, earn-outs are heavily weighted in the buyer's favor. You, as the seller, may agree to terms that appear reasonable during negotiation because they resemble what you've experienced up to that point. However, you don't have the experience of strategic thinking about potential future impact and thus can't imagine a situation where the deal won't work out as designed. From the seller's perspective, an earn-out is often challenging because the seller will have no control over the business during the future period when the earn-out is paid. Thus, the seller must rely on the good faith of the buyer along with the achievement of the metric which triggers the earn-out—areas over which you have no control. While an earn-out appears to favor the buyer, sellers have other alternatives such as owner financing, consulting agreements, or other contractual means to facilitate a transaction that works to benefit both buyer and seller.

The team is designed to give you a superior return, often realized in less time spent negotiating and superior deal terms. Your team will have a strategy and will have predetermined what's in your best interest.

A superior return will factor in the tax impact of the deal. Ultimately, what really matters is how much you get to keep after all expenses and taxes. Your team will maximize that amount and accomplish the goal.

> *Ultimately, what really matters is how much*
> *you get to keep after all expenses and taxes.*

It's not hard to assemble your team. Talk to your current advisors (accountants, bankers, attorneys) and ask if they have experience in the transaction process. If they have minimal or no experience, then ask them for referrals to those who do have good experience. The key is to gather folks together who specialize in the transaction process. Set an introductory meeting with these new contacts to review their experience and competence and to find out if you'd enjoy working with them. Only hire someone if there's chemistry, competence, and experience.

3. Assessment

Your team of experts will deliver a comprehensive assessment that incorporates the position of the seller and the anticipated perception of the buyer. This is key to positioning the business opportunity in the most favorable light.

The assessment looks at all facets of the business:

- **Financial:** Are the records in place? Are they pertinent? Do they clearly and accurately reflect the benefit of possessing the business? Are they easily understood by an outsider? Are they reflective of what's being offered? How do they compare to the industry? What are the trends? What are the drivers?

- **Products:** What does the business sell? What's the range of products? What's the price of the products? What's the price history of the products? What's the gross margin?

- **People:** Are there key people in the business? What's the tenure of the staff? What's the turnover rate? What's the compensation? How does the business attract staff?

- **Systems and processes:** What systems and processes are in place? What's the customer acquisition process? What's the customer fulfillment process? What's the internal working process?

- **Market:** In what industry and sector does the business operate? What's the market size? What's the available market? What are the trends of the market?

- **Dependence:** Is the business dependent on any one person, supplier, or customer?

- **Customers:** How many customers does the business serve? How does it rank in terms of customer satisfaction? What's the range of products delivered to each customer?

- **Owner impact:** What does the owner do? What impact would a change of owner have?

The list above covers the major categories and their key aspects. The assessment is designed to perform a SWOT analysis: strengths, weaknesses, opportunities, and threats of the business in its current market.

A DIY seller usually carries this information in their head, but they don't take the time to record and analyze it. They often think they'll share the information with the right buyer at the right time, which is precisely the wrong way to approach buyers.

> *Don't think you're the only one assessing your business. The buyers are doing the same thing, and DIY sellers aren't often prepared to respond to a buyer's assessment of their business.*

Don't think you're the only one assessing your business. The buyers are doing the same thing, and DIY sellers aren't often prepared to respond to a buyer's assessment of their business. They don't know how. They're also commonly offended by inquiries and questions, and they allow their emotions to cloud their response. This can quickly kill a deal.

When you surround yourself with an experienced team, they will review the assessment long before a buyer gets involved. The team will work through the strengths and weaknesses and agree to a plan to address them. If there isn't time to fix or correct a weakness, the team will evaluate its impact and provide for that in the offering, which will neutralize the possibility of a buyer using that against you to reduce the price.

It may take a few weeks to gather all the information and typically a few more weeks to put the information into a format where a thorough review can occur. Armed with a good assessment, the team is ready to move to the next phase.

4. Informational Documents

These are the documents that will be shared with prospective buyers to illustrate your business being offered for sale. The business type, the market served, and its history will determine the complete range and depth of the documents, but there are several standard documents we'll explore.

Most businesses don't hang a "FOR SALE" sign when the owner is ready to move on. You probably don't want your current customers, employees, and suppliers to be aware of the transaction process until it's complete. You also don't want a prospective buyer talking about the business being for sale within their industry or market segment. For these reasons and more, it's standard practice to first share a Non-Disclosure Agreement (NDA) with a potential buyer.

An NDA determines who a potential buyer can talk to regarding the details of the business for sale. It's an enforceable agreement and has some teeth and is designed to underscore the serious damage that can occur if the parties don't honor the agreement. Experienced brokers and advisors will come prepared to customize a template agreement to match your needs as the seller.

After a potential buyer agrees and signs the NDA, they'll receive information that identifies your specific business and its operating characteristics. This information will often include a summary document known as a flyer or brochure. This document will be concise and have one or more pertinent facts designed to entice the buyer to seek additional information. It will focus on benefits and will position the business in the best possible light.

A Confidential Information Memorandum (CIM) is one of the most comprehensive documents prepared. It's designed to be an executive summary of your business and will touch on each of the eight main characteristics covered in the assessment document. This document is, by design, objective. It highlights strengths of the business, which provides the prospective buyer with a solid overview of the opportunity.

The CIM includes many business-specific summaries of the financial statements, business system, and process overviews. These documents provide a comprehensive view of what happens both publicly and behind the scenes of your company. They provide a lot of information but don't include any trade secrets or special proprietary information that could give a competitor a strategic advantage. The goal is to provide the prospective buyer with enough information for them to deliver a formal response indicating their interest in acquiring your business.

Many times, a prospective buyer will review the CIM and then ask for supporting documents to help them understand more about a specific aspect of the business. For example, they may want to understand how dependent the business is on its customers, so they might ask for a list of customers ranked by the proportion of sales revenue each customer represents. These supporting documents are normal and customary but must be prepared in a way that will satisfy the buyer without divulging trade secrets. It is appropriate to share additional details to get to a deal stage, but much of this type of activity occurs during the diligence period.

Your broker or advisor will lead the team to produce the required information and then restate it in a format familiar to the widest audience of buyers. Time to complete this documentation is varied. It depends on how long it takes you to provide the required information and the time it takes the advisory team to format it appropriately. For a business producing less than fifty million in annual revenue, this process can normally be completed in a short period of time.

You'll find more information about informational documents in chapters 6 and 8.

5. Marketing

A lot of time and energy went into identifying and selecting the right team, assessing the business, and building the informational documents. Now it's time to put all that effort to work.

The first step is to set the target by developing the ideal buyer profile. In building the profile, the goal is to answer the following question: "Who will pay the most because they'll get the biggest benefit from acquiring this business?"

Often the answer is a strategic buyer—a buyer who can gain market share, product range, additional location, or another aspect complimentary to their existing business. Occasionally, one might target a technical expert, a craftsperson, or other lifestyle buyer who may generate the highest value by achieving a specific individual objective. But in all instances, you want to make sure the marketing plan and informational documents speak to the financial buyer, the buyer whose first consideration is the investment characteristics of the business opportunity.

Once your team has an ideal buyer profile, they can put their research tools to work and locate those buyers. Then it's simply a matter of reaching out to them and engaging them in a dialogue to determine who's interested and capable of buying the business.

6. Diligence

Once a buyer has been located and has enough information to make an offer, the next step is for them to convey their offer in written format. A Letter of Intent (LOI) is the most prevalent format.

The LOI is a written communication from the buyer to the seller expressing a desire to purchase, the terms under which they intend to complete the transaction, and the timeframe they expect it will take. A LOI may include many additional terms. It's commonly a non-binding document, which means either party can walk away under certain circumstances. The LOI begins to set the rules for the time between delivery of the purchase engagement and the closing, which is commonly referred to as the diligence period. This is the time between the offer and the signing of the closing documents that the buyer takes to learn and verify specific pertinent facts regarding your business in order to affect the transfer. Buyers normally deliver a list of things they want to see and do before they'll close. You, the seller, are responsible for responding to the buyer's needs (and potentially the needs of the buyer's lender).

There's a common perception in the market that buyers use this time to discover weakness in a business, so they can negotiate down the price. While this does occur, a prepared seller with an assembled team rarely experiences this problem. You'll be well served to disclose everything about the business and prepare explanations where necessary to help mitigate the weaknesses of the business. If you've worked through this with your team, you're prepared to discuss all aspects of the business, and you've already accounted for any weaknesses in their asking price. On the other hand, DIY sellers often experience this problem. They aren't prepared when a buyer uses this tactic. When the advantage shifts to the buyer, price is often sacrificed.

You'll be well served to disclose everything about the business and prepare explanations where necessary to help mitigate the weaknesses of the business.

The team approach really earns its keep during the diligence stage. The upfront investment pays off because the team approach accomplishes two primary goals:

1. Keeps all parties on task – Diligence is a very detailed and intense process and often involves many people on both the buyer and seller side of the transaction.

Experienced brokers and advisors are responsible for keeping all parties on task and accountable for specific activities and outcomes.

2. Honor the timeline – Time equals money when it comes to the input and impact of the various team members. Keeping everyone on task and on time results in lower transaction costs.

For a cash buyer and a seller who's working with a team, diligence can literally be done in a matter of days. If a lender is providing a portion of the funds for a buyer and if you have a team, it's normal for diligence to last much longer. But for a DIY seller, it's common for that period to extend way beyond ninety days.

7. Closing

The end is in sight! So much information has been shared, the negotiation is over, and now all that's left is signing the papers and transferring the money. Well, that's the way it's supposed to work. However, it's not always the case.

Closing is often a fire drill where all parties frantically take one last look through every document and representation and make sure all the i's are dotted and all the t's are crossed.

The market is littered with stories of everything falling apart at the last second. And many of these stories are true—most often with DIY sellers.

The market is littered with stories of everything falling apart at the last second. And many of these stories are true—most often with DIY sellers. Why? Generally because expectations and emotions are high, and both sides realize that the buyer holds all the cards. So, if the buyer doesn't get what they want, they walk. Sellers hate being held hostage.

It doesn't have to be that way. Sellers with a team have experience on their side, and experience teaches them to read the signs for approaching hazards. The experience again demonstrates its value in the closing stage. The team can spot warning signs and know how to keep everyone focused on the desired outcome—a smooth business transfer. It's trite but true: as long as everyone stays focused on the goal, the goal gets achieved.

Closing dates involve both parties signing the final papers and verifying funds wired (most common method of money transfer). In a properly managed transaction, the agreements will have been reviewed and agreed upon (and more often even signed) before the closing date. All the necessary licenses, permits, or transfers have taken place (or are scheduled to take place on the appropriate date), and all verifications are in place. Funds have been verified on deposit and scheduled for wire transfer. Notices are prepared, and if employees aren't aware, an all-hands meeting is scheduled. Customer communications and press releases are reviewed, approved, and ready for disbursement. All systems are "GO."

Then it's time to inform the employees, suppliers, and customers. It works best if both you and the buyer make these announcements together and in person. The buyer should be prepared to address what, if any, changes will take place for employees, including job responsibilities, reporting, compensation, benefits, and so on. Suppliers may require renewed credit detail and supply specifics. Customers (particularly those who are strategic or represent a significant share of sales) will often want to know that things like price, delivery, and performance will remain satisfactory, and they often want to understand the new owner's vision of the future. Preparing for this announcement will go a long way to ensure a smooth transition.

Mark was ready for the marketing launch to sell his business. He and his team scheduled a ninety-day marketing process with a contingency to expand it by up to sixty days if they didn't get the interest desired. They were already putting all anticipated due diligence documentation into a data vault and anticipated that a thorough diligence period would take no more than ninety days. Everything was designed to consummate with their fiscal year end to get the best advantage for the seller. All systems were "GO."

Bill, however, was wearing down. He'd started many months ago and all he had to show for it was increased pressure on his business and on his mind. He began to think of simply closing the doors before he was forced to close. He thought he could get a job to pay off his business debt. Almost a year after he'd spotted the trouble, Bill was running out of options and resources, and he was no closer to his goal of selling than when he'd begun.

Bill clearly wasn't himself, and he wore the pressure like an ill-fitting suit. A relative noticed his obvious strain and called him on it. Bill confided his troubles, and he was reminded that they had a family friend who was a business consultant.

WHO BUYS BUSINESSES?

You might be wondering who would buy your business. The answer is that *it depends*; it depends on what the business is and how it's performing.

As explained in chapter 2, there are at least three types of buyers.

1. Lifestyle buyers

2. Economic buyers

3. Strategic buyers

These buyer types can be individuals or other companies. Motivations vary from type to type, and the ideal business fit is different for each buyer. The buyer's motivations are key to understanding how to engage with them. It also helps to understand what they value most in a transaction and how they'll gauge the offer price in relation to what they're willing to pay.

> *Motivations vary from type to type,*
> *and the ideal business fit is different for*
> *each buyer.*

1. Lifestyle/Entrepreneurial Buyers

The lifestyle buyer makes up the largest pool of available buyers in any market. Typically an individual person, these buyers represent the bulk of in-bound inquiries from an advertisement for a business opportunity. Generally speaking, these buyers want to work for themselves, they have some money saved, and they're seeking an ideal opportunity. As the world becomes more connected, people from every corner of the globe now have access to see and respond to opportunities to acquire businesses.

Their specific motivations may vary, but these people are looking for an opportunity to work without having to report to a boss. And yet when I talk to them, I often find they don't have any actual experience working for themselves. It's the *idea* of working for themselves that they find so compelling.

Generally, lifestyle buyers set their sights within their own experiences. Thus, if they currently make $50,000 per year, they seek a business opportunity that allows them to make a low multiple of that—perhaps $150,000 per year. They think that the answer to their prayers will be having a multiple of their current earnings plus the freedom to work for themselves.

Ultimately, this vision provides them the lifestyle of their dreams. That's why I refer to them as lifestyle buyers; they seek to find a business opportunity that will give them the lifestyle they desire.

The *entrepreneurial* buyer is a variation of this buyer type. Like the lifestyle buyer, their scope and vision are restricted to their experience. However, they often have the added dimension of working for another company in the same industry. Because of this experience, they usually have the strong belief that they have the entrepreneurial drive to do the job better than the company they work for. These buyers have some savings or equity they can access, and if they find the right opportunity, they know they can innovate something compelling and prosper.

There's another variation on this same theme—the *technical expert* or *craftsman* buyer. Similar to the others, they have a limited scope and ability but may have a deep knowledge or skill set that differentiates them. Again, they seek an opportunity where they can work without a boss.

Individuals in this buyer classification do buy businesses. But they do so infrequently and rarely more than once. They have money to spend and can make time around their work and life schedule to investigate opportunities, but they have a hard time finding the right opportunity. They're the window shoppers of the transaction universe and will spend a tremendous amount of time following their dream of how a process should work, but they have little knowledge of or experience in actually completing transactions.

2. Economic Buyers

There has been explosive growth in this category of buyers. They can be either private individuals or entities, and they have the money to buy. They generally fall into three subcategories and are all motivated by the opportunity to put their money (or fund money) to work to generate a return.

> *The explosive growth in this category has come from the recent development of the first subcategory of financial buyers known as private equity.*

The explosive growth in this category has come from the recent development of the first subcategory of financial buyers known as *private equity*. These entities are made up of partners and managers. The partners are individuals with money and expertise in a particular business classification.

The partners pool their money, leverage their expertise and contacts, and seek to accelerate the growth of a company, thereby multiplying the enterprise value of the company. The partners deploy managers to oversee the businesses they invest in to generate economies of scale by using similar systems and processes across their organization. As of this writing, it's estimated that there are more than 10,000 entities of this type in the USA, and that number is growing.

If a private equity organization has raised a fund of capital to invest, then they'll have a particular time period in which to put their capital to work and a specific period to hold the entities they acquire. Generally, the private equity companies buy and hold a company for five to seven years, then sell it with the goal of realizing a minimum pre-determined return on their capital. Funds within these entities are quite specific in their investment criteria and quickly determine whether or not a deal meets these criteria.

These buyers are often very astute and have an experienced transaction team. Transactions are their main focus (both buying and selling) with a hold period in between. These experienced teams often overwhelm DIY sellers and provide a real challenge for sellers. Private equity entities evaluate many opportunities and quickly and grow bored or pass on an opportunity that might be ideal for them if the DIY seller can't produce information on the buyer's timetable and in a familiar format.

Private equity buyers are extremely transparent about their motivations. Buyers in this field even advertise the ideal fit for them and describe it in terms of the business operation and the financial performance desired. Private equity buyers may even have salespeople working for them that actively solicit other transaction professionals and use sophisticated tools to surface ideal candidates for them.

The second subcategory is known as *private investment*. Warren Buffet is the poster child for this type of entity. He uses his original company, Berkshire Hathaway, as a means to purchase particular businesses. Unlike private equity companies, private investment companies often invest money attributed to one specific entity or individual (versus pooling funds), and private investment buyers also purchase with the intention to hold or own indefinitely. Private equity must sell at some point in the future, but private investment has no such mandate.

Both buyer types are also similar in certain ways. Both openly discuss their motivation for purchase, and both closely evaluate the opportunity based on financial return. The private investment entity may have different return criteria but are often open and transparent about what they expect. A big difference is that private investment buyers don't use debt to purchase a business—they don't borrow funds. Buyers of this type typically purchase on a cash basis and want to own one hundred percent of a company.

They're also very astute buyers. They evaluate hundreds of opportunities and invest in relatively few. They look for a specific set of criteria and won't waste your time window-shopping the deal. They'll respond promptly and will make offers and close deals as quickly as possible.

The third subcategory is the *private investor*. This is typically a private individual who invests their own personal money. Their motivation is similar to the others, and they primarily buy and hold a business. Investors of this type typically pay cash and like to own one hundred percent of the entity they acquire. The primary difference here is that they may only hold a single entity at a time—not multiple companies.

3. Strategic Buyers

This type of buyer can be an individual or a company. Strategic buyers are interested in purchasing for a specific outcome that will enhance their current business. Strategic buyers often stretch and pay more than a financial or lifestyle buyer because, typically, they'll receive an immediate and outsized benefit from the purchase.

> *Strategic buyers will often stretch and pay more than a financial or lifestyle buyer because, typically, they'll receive an immediate and outsized benefit from the purchase.*

Their motivations can be any of the following:

- Add a complementary or line extension to their product portfolio
- Add a location
- Add a range of products or services
- Add sales capability
- Eliminate a competitor from the marketplace
- Add technology or capability
- Remove or reduce fixed or variable cost

And this just begins to explain their motivations. In general, the combination of what Strategic buyers already have plus the opportunity the seller provides equals more than they can build on their own. It's a $1+1= >2$ equation.

Strategic buyers are often experienced at acquisitions and may follow a specific formula. They generally have a team of transaction experts and will move quickly to get a transaction done. They're often motivated to act and close before competitors or peers in the market have the opportunity

Bill was not aware of it, but at the time he was scrambling to sell his company there were several strategic buyers considering deals in his industry. And Bill was an excellent fit for many of them. Even though Bill was struggling, his industry was consolidating, and

his business was ideally positioned to benefit. But Bill didn't have a team to direct him toward these opportunities, so he almost missed the chance to get a deal done.

Mark's team was actively pursuing all three types of buyers. They researched and highlighted those that best fit from a strategic perspective, and Mark enjoyed the exercise of analyzing his competitors to determine the most probable fits. His team also put together a prospectus for the financial buyers and actively targeted those whose ideal profile best matched Mark's business model. They even put together some targeted advertising to attract an appropriate entrepreneurial buyer.

Further, Mark's team contracted with an industry-specific advisor to consult on a particular aspect of the proposed transaction. Although it added some expense to the front of the transaction, this additional assessment was quickly justified, as most of the interested buyers requested the specific data that the contracted analysis delivered. This became a nominal expense in light of the total transaction and yielded an exceptional return on investment to the transaction.

Mark's activities yielded more than fifty inquires with more than fifteen offers to purchase. Because of the high level of interest and effectiveness of their campaign, Mark and his team extended the marketing period to get the highest and best offers.

WHAT BUYERS LOOK FOR IN A BUSINESS

Bill finally scheduled a meeting with the consultant his family member recommended. He was anxious about the meeting because he assumed the consultant would want to sell him something, and he didn't have the funds, regardless of how good the offer might be. Bill received a short list of items the consultant needed to see regarding his business, and Bill was embarrassed that his financial documents weren't current.

Mark was also busy—busy locating documents and loading them into the data vault. He had met with several potential buyers, and his team had built a FAQ (frequently asked questions) document to keep track of every query tossed their way. The team worked great together, and Mark was continually impressed with how well the process was going.

MARKETING PROCESS

Buyers are hungry for information. No matter the motivation, they want a well-rounded view of the business opportunity, the market, and the business's experience serving its

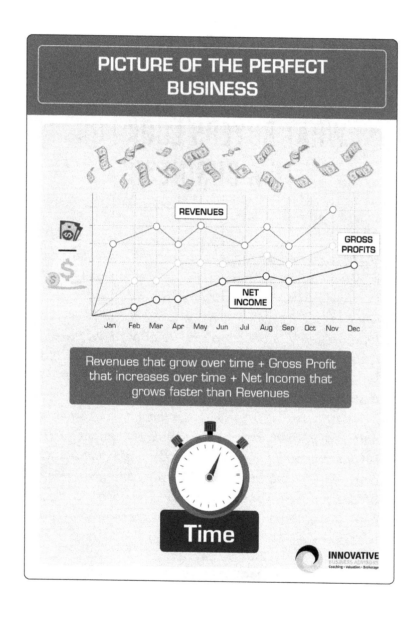

market. But there's always one question that comes first: "Why is the business for sale?"

> *Buyers are hungry for information. No matter the motivation, they want a well-rounded view of the business opportunity, the market, and the business's experience serving its market.*

Buyers first want to understand the circumstances surrounding the business opportunity. It's an incredibly important consideration for both parties, so it's critically important for sellers to answer this first question truthfully and in a manner that will attract buyers.

Once the ideal buyer profile is identified, you can build a marketing process designed to attract this type of buyer. If you speak to their motivations, there are always ways to define the attractive components of the business opportunity around the benefits the ideal buyer would receive. That's the essence of the marketing program—identifying the appropriate buyer type and then drafting the marketing documents that speak their language.

SPECIFIC DATA

Because buyers look at many opportunities, they see a wide variety of viewpoints. The most impactful format is to focus on the facts.

Buyers need to know an abundance of details about a business. After buyers agree to keep the information confidential, the buyer will know the full name of your business, the contact information, the year it was formed, the state of incorporation, the type of business entity, the ownership structure, its hours of operation, the number of employees, its DBAs, its trademarks and other intellectual property, whether you own or lease your premises, and so on. These facts give the buyer the information they need to decide if they want to pursue the opportunity.

Of course, they expect to see a complete set of financial documents, including all operating reports and tax returns. Be sure to call out specific operating metrics and ratios and clearly detail the cash flow of the business. If there are industry standard valuations metrics, it's helpful to illustrate those as well, particularly when the business looks better than the industry norms.

Details regarding employees are a key area of sensitivity. Buyers are entitled to know how many employees currently work at a business, the mix of full-time and part-time employees, if there's a representation agreement in place for the employees or a portion thereof, and any specific operating metrics, such as average wage and tenure. If there are key employees, it's important to note whether they're employed on an at-will basis or if they're covered by an employment agreement. Employee benefit programs are usually illustrated, and representation documents may include an employee manual if the business has a current program in place.

Of course, the product or service details are explained along with pricing and other pertinent details. It's critical to refrain from divulging trade secrets here or providing any level of detail a competitor could use, but there does need to be sufficient detail to enable a buyer to understand how the business competes with its products or services. The history of pricing comes up quite often, as buyers want to understand the normal cadence the business follows to adjust price with their customers. If there are key suppliers or vendors for the products or services, the buyers will want to know details regarding those relationships.

DIY sellers rarely disclose information about legal actions upfront. This can be an early deal breaker as buyers want to know if the company has been involved in legal actions in the past, are currently involved, or have any threatened legal action facing them. And buyers will routinely run a search to determine if the company is party to any suit. If they discover a lawsuit and the seller has not disclosed it, the buyers will become very cautious. The same is true for environmental issues for those businesses where this may be a concern.

Buyers want to see the assets that are included in the transaction. It's important to detail current assets and fixed long-term assets, whether or not they have any remaining book value. It's a good practice to include a photo log of primary fixed assets and provide those representations throughout the marketing process. Buyers enjoy seeing these pictures because it gives them a glance at the type of property and its general condition. This is particularly true if there's real property involved.

The systems and processes a business uses are also important components of the marketing package. If the business uses a specific technology, it's always good to detail that along with the version and renewal details. If there are any internet-enabled portals, particularly e-commerce, buyers will want to know all the details surrounding those areas.

Finally, it's a good practice to include an overview of the market. If possible, a summary of your key competitors, target customers, and specific areas for growth, whether planned or unplanned, help buyers understand how the company competes. This can be critical with highly-specialized businesses.

Taken together, all of this information gives the potential buyer a solid overview of the business opportunity. When they finish the review, the buyer should understand the business and will ask specific clarifying questions.

Taken together, all of this information gives the potential buyer a solid overview of the business opportunity. When they finish the review, the buyer should understand the business and will ask specific clarifying questions. This is the perfect time to *listen*. Listen carefully, so you can understand what's most important for the buyer. You should try to answer the buyer's questions as fully and truthfully as possible without divulging trade secrets. A buyer has the right to ask for everything, so never try to hide a defect because it will ultimately be discovered.

CHAPTER
7

WHAT IS YOUR BUSINESS WORTH?

Before Mark had the conversation with his attorney and accountant, he'd calculated what he thought his business was worth and how much he would need to lead the life he desired after the sale. He was conservative in his calculation but firm in his conviction. The broker ran the valuation, and the low end of the range was twenty percent higher than Mark had thought it would be. He was pleased to see the larger number, but he wouldn't allow himself to get too excited until actual offers came in.

Bill, however, had established his number solely on anecdotal information about what he'd heard over time. His calculation involved adding up what he'd invested in the business over time, and then he attempted to discount that amount for the current value of the equipment. After all, Bill reasoned, the equipment cost equaled what the banks had loaned him. He assumed that if a buyer needed financing, their bank would do the same and they would calculate the value of the equipment.

No one seemed interested in buying Bill's business. So, he reduced his price for each new prospective buyer. It quickly fell to a price point that wouldn't allow Bill to cover his obligations. Still, he reasoned that covering most of his obligation was better than closing the business and still being responsible for all its debt. In Bill's mind, his asking price had some relation to the worth of the business, but he had no idea how it related to value of the business.

WHAT'S THE DIFFERENCE BETWEEN VALUE, WORTH, AND PRICE?

Before jumping into calculating value, you must first understand what you're evaluating. In ordinary conversation, the terms *value, worth,* and *price* are often used interchangeably. But by definition—and when talking about the valuation of a business—they have entirely different meanings. Value defines the estimated monetary "worth" of the entity. But what really matters is "Fair Market Value" which defines what the business is worth in the current market conditions.

> *In ordinary conversation, the terms value, worth, and price are often used interchangeably. But by definition—and when talking about the valuation of a business—they have entirely different meanings.*

The Internal Revenue Service (IRS) defines fair market value as set forth in Revenue Ruling 59-60 as follows:

"The price at which the property would change hands between a willing buyer and a willing seller when the former is not under any compulsion to buy and the latter is not under any compulsion to sell, both parties having reasonable knowledge of the relevant facts."

In the business world, *fair market value* is the term most often used in relation to value.

Fair Market Value:

- Is hypothetical and doesn't address actual individuals in a real transaction
- Is subject to differing opinions and judgements
- Cannot be proven by actual sale transactions

Worth:

- Is a judgment of the value of a business to a real buyer and/or seller
- Does not necessarily address an *arms-length* transaction. *Arms-length* means neither the buyer nor seller are under any compulsion to buy/sell, and both are acting based on reasonable knowledge of the facts involved.
- Takes into account personal circumstances, emotions, preferences, and limitations of the parties involved—all of which usually make worth different from the ideal fair market value
- Can be confirmed by the outcome of an actual transaction because the goal was to estimate what two individuals (or groups) would pay/accept for a particular business

Price:

- Is directly connected to worth via the process of negotiation and can be confirmed

When a sale is contemplated, the seller starts by considering the asking price. The selling price is where the buyer and seller end up—based on their individual judgments of worth and their skills as negotiators—in combination with the particular pressures that push them toward buying and selling.

You know your customers, the products and services, and how best to market them. But do you know how much your business is actually worth?

As a business owner, you've poured your heart and soul into your company. You know your customers, the products and services, and how best to market them. But do you know how much your business is actually worth? The fact is, many business owners don't, so when the numbers are finally crunched, the results can be surprising—in both good ways and bad!

WHAT DETERMINES THE VALUE OF A BUSINESS?

Professionals who perform business valuations use the most frequently cited basis for valuing closely-held (privately owned) businesses: IRS Revenue Ruling 59-60 (portions noted above). The IRS uses this set of guidelines to determine the value of closely-held stock in gift and estate cases. The ruling outlines several factors for consideration:

- The history and nature of the business
- The economics of the industry
- Book value and financial condition of the business
- Earnings and dividend paying capacities of the business
- Goodwill and other intangibles
- Sales of stock and proportion of the total stock to be valued

The ruling discusses the significance of earnings and assets. But it doesn't prescribe any hard and fast formulas. It advises: "A sound valuation will be based upon all relevant facts . . . common sense, informed judgment, and reasonableness."

THE TRUE TEST OF VALUE

In day-to-day business operations of sales and mergers, the cornerstone of valuation is based on good old-fashioned math. Prospective buyers invest in businesses for one reason: to generate earnings (profit). Expectations of profit vary based on the degree of investment risk. The higher the risk, the higher the expected profit demanded. Buyers are interested in hard and fast numbers.

Investors invest in businesses for one reason: to generate earnings (profit).

Accountants and bankers often use a simple formula: they take the value of the assets and subtract the value of the liabilities to find the net asset value of a business. This is commonly referred to as *book value*. In other words, you take what you own, subtract what you owe, and what's left is what the business is worth. At least, according to the balance sheet.

There is also another component of value known as *goodwill*. Goodwill is the premium a company pays when it buys another company for more than its book value. For the acquirer, this becomes an intangible asset which may represent the value of the acquired company's brand name, customer base, employees, technology, knowledge base, or cashflow. The difference between the purchase price, non-compete agreements, etc. and book value defined above is recorded as the "goodwill" in the assets section of the balance sheet for the buyer.

You can also hire someone to do an independent valuation or appraisal for a more thorough determination of the value of your company. The scope, detail, and cost of a business valuation vary widely based on the size and complexity of the business, the purpose of the valuation, and the organization doing the valuation.

METHODS TO CALCULATE VALUE

The *asset method* and *earnings method* are the two basic financial methods for valuing a private business. Both methods use two primary financial statements of the business: the balance sheet and the income statement. To set the foundation to begin your own valuation, determine the method most relevant to your business.

The Asset Method

The asset method focuses on business performance metrics recorded and reported on the balance sheet. There are four specific asset-based methods that arrive at a value for a business:

1. **Book Value:** Book value (also called net worth or owner's equity) is the total assets minus the total liabilities. The book value is what the business owns minus what it owes.

Book value usually only represents liquid assets (easily convertible to cash) and reflects their current market value. So, if the majority of assets are *not* liquid assets, you need to adjust the book value to come closer to fair market value.

2. **Adjusted Book Value:** Differences between book value and market value usually arise in *property and equipment* and *intangibles and goodwill.*

The IRS requires plant and equipment (fixed assets) to be carried on the books at original cost and depreciated over allowable recovery periods. These periods vary according to the prevailing tax law at the time the asset was purchased. As a rule, this is often shorter than the asset's actual productive life in the business. This difference results in a rapid write-off of assets, which is shown as depreciation on the income statement.

Frequently, investments in equipment are virtually eliminated from the balance sheet through depreciation, even though the assets are still in operation. The same is true of buildings and improvements, which in the real world often appreciate rather than depreciate. Because of these accounting practices, depreciated book values generally understate the fair market value of fixed assets in the current marketplace.

Additionally, intangible assets and goodwill only appear on the balance sheet if they have a cost basis. That is, if they appear recorded at a value equal to what it actually cost to acquire them. If nothing was paid to acquire them, then they don't show up. But these assets can, of course, play a vital role in the value of a company. Intangibles may include specific assets like patents, copyrights, trademarks, client lists, and trade contracts, or even more immaterial assets like a good reputation or a strong market position. A business often accumulates intangible assets over its lifetime.

Whether assets are tangible or intangible, they need to be written up (or down) to their fair market value present at the time the valuation is performed. That way, the asset-based value of the business (adjusted assets minus adjusted liabilities) can be calculated. Calculating these adjustments delivers adjusted book value.

3.   **Liquidation Value:** This method of valuation does not consider the business as an ongoing operation. It assumes the business will cease operating and close, selling its assets and paying its liabilities. Any leftover cash will go to the owners.

This calculation is only meaningful in setting the absolute bottom price. This is the price at which an owner would be better off liquidating their company rather than selling. The liquidation value takes into account the fact that the assets (inventory, property, and equipment) will bring in less money because they are sold under pressure.

Here are some general rules of thumb to use for discounting the value of assets during an immediate liquidation or sale under pressure:

25% discount of all accounts receivable < 90 days old

75% discount of all accounts receivable > 90 days old

50% discount of all inventory

60% discount of the current market value of equipment

75% discount of the current market value of buildings

60% discount of the current market value of land

100% discount for all leasehold improvements

4. **Reproduction Value:** This is the converse of liquidation value. This value is the current market cost of reproducing the fixed assets of the business (inventory, property, and equipment) in today's market. Like liquidation value, reproduction value only represents a benchmark—the value that a buyer would not exceed unless the earnings of the business dictated it for other reasons.

These four asset value models are the most often used methods to determine the value of a business based on the value of its assets. For an ongoing business, these are also the least used methods to determine the value of the business. Asset value models are most useful when liquidation is being contemplated.

But what about that item noted in the last section—earnings?

The Earnings Method

A strong argument can be made that a business is worth what it earns, not what it owns. The earnings method focuses on business performance items measured and recorded on the income statement. The real value of any business in this case is its earning power—the ability to produce profits in the future based on what it has produced in the past. The earnings approach is founded on the theory that a business should yield a fair return on the owner's capital invested in the business.

For valuation purposes, both *earnings* and *fair return* need to be defined.

What Are Earnings?

For most closely held private businesses, earnings (commonly called E.B.I.T.D.A. = *earnings before interest, taxes, depreciation and amortization*) are defined as a combination of:

1. The accounting net profit or net income

   PLUS (+)

2. Excess owner's salary—the amount an owner-manager pays themselves above the amount the owner would pay to hire general manager for the same job. This applies to small businesses, defined as businesses having less than $500,000 in annual sales. The entire owner's salary is generally added back to the accounting net profit to compute adjusted earnings.

   PLUS (+)

3. Depreciation and amortization expense (non-cash expense items)

   PLUS (+)

4. Interest expense

   PLUS (+)

5. Extraordinary one-time expenses that are not recurring

   PLUS (+)

6. Any excess discretionary expenses that incur solely to the owner's benefit

A special note on discretionary expenses: business owners usually want to increase their salaries (a tax deduction for the corporation) and credit the company with as many discretionary items like customer entertainment or business promotion as possible as a way to hold down the company's before-tax income. In contrast, buyers want to see the total cashflow the business produces—including earnings they can use at their own discretion if they purchase the company. In other words, it's all about the actual profits/cash-flow and not tax advantaged accounting practices. Therefore, earnings must be normalized to reflect the actual return on investment to the owner.

There are several ways to forecast earnings. They're all based on the premise that if past or current earnings indicate future earnings, then they can be used to value the business. Stated another way, the value of the company can be based on what it will earn in the future as opposed to what it produced in the past. However, past earnings do provide the basic data on which to base future earnings projections.

Past earnings can be used in different forms to calculate value:

1. Average earnings (for three to five years)

2. Weighted average earnings (for three to five years)

3. Current (or most recent) earnings

Determine and then select which of these most accurately reflect the earnings the company is expected to produce in the future.

What Is a Fair Return?

Fair return is commonly known as rate-of-return or capitalization rate.

The earnings available to the owner of a business represent a return on the funds that have been invested in the business. In simple terms, the initial capital stock plus retained earnings. If a buyer were to invest $100,000 in a business and wanted a 20 percent return on investment, the business would need to produce $20,000 per year in earnings:

$100,000 × 20% = $20,000

On the other hand, if a business produced $20,000 in earnings per year and a prospective buyer required a 20 percent return on investment, they would, in theory, invest $100,000 in the business:

$20,000 / 20% = $100,000

Stated another way, the value of a business that produces $20,000 in earnings per year is $100,000 for a buyer that requires a 20 percent return on investment. In this example, the 20 percent is the capitalization rate and it's equivalent to the required return on investment on earnings. Capitalization rates are commonly used to determine the value of a business based on earnings.

ADJUSTING FOR RISK AND RETURN

As noted earlier, the higher the risk of an investment, the higher the required return. A buyer will normally require a higher rate of return on investment from a business perceived or proven to be higher in risk. Buyers will use the past performance of a business to gauge the riskiness of the earnings. If the earnings bounce around and are routinely variable, the buyer will apply a higher level of risk in their calculations. The capitalization rates for risky businesses are therefore higher than those for less risky businesses.

The higher the risk of an investment, the higher the required return. A buyer will normally require a higher rate of return on investment from a business perceived or proven to be higher in risk.

The formula for determining the value of a private business based on earnings is:

Value = Earnings (average, weighted, or current) x
Capitalization Rate (risk rate)

The capitalization rate is the inverse of a multiple of
earnings: A cap rate of 20 percent equals a multiple of 5.
Using the previous example:

Earnings: $20,000
Times Multiple: x5
Equals Value: $100,000

DISCOUNTED FUTURE EARNINGS AND COMPARABLE PUBLIC COMPANIES

If the future earnings of a business are not expected to look
like past earnings, then discounting those future earnings to
find their present value is a valid method of valuation.

For example, the business may have a patent on a product or service that's scheduled to expire in the next year or
two. When the patent expires, the business anticipates the
price will need to be adjusted, which will change the gross
sales and margin the company receives on that product or
service. This could have a detrimental impact on earnings
and should be accounted for in the valuation.

This method is frequently rejected because of its sub-
jectivity in actual buy-sell transactions. In the sale of small
businesses (defined as those with sales revenue < two million annually), it's rarely used.

Another method is comparing with publicly traded
companies to arrive at a guideline for a price to earnings
multiple, but it's rarely used with most private businesses.
Why? There's a vast difference between the control, scope,
management, and tax ramifications of having an individual
majority-owner in a private business versus those that exist
in a publicly held companies.

A combination of asset-based methods and earn-
ings-based methods is the most common way to determine

the financial value of an independent business. As you've probably noted, these methods can, and usually do, produce a widely varying range of values.

OTHER FACTORS THAT INFLUENCE VALUE

We've explored the various methods for determining the financial value of a business. This is the cornerstone of the valuation, and for financial buyers, it'll be the primary (and perhaps the only) valuation process they use. There are other factors that also affect value, which may be among the most important factors for different buyer types.

For example, does the seller own the real estate where the business is housed? This is a common factor that influences value. Generally speaking, large companies, private equity, and private investment groups don't want to acquire real estate along with a business. The issue of who continues to own the real estate can muddy the sale process.

My experience is that buyers always start with financial value and then progress to evaluate various factors that impact that value. I use The Value Builder System®, an excellent methodology for business owners of all sizes to evaluate the true enterprise value of their business. Let's take a look at those additional factors.

Growth Value

The potential for growth can be a key value driver for certain buyer types. In the financial calculations noted above, this could be reflected in the discounted value of future earnings. Imagine a business is on the cusp of releasing a new product or beginning to serve a new contract. The future revenue growth of the business is forecast to be impacted by 20 percent or more, a percentage of growth realized by less than two percent of American companies. This strong amount of growth is a key value driver for strategic buyers and should therefore be accounted for in the worth calculation of the business.

8 Drivers of Company Value

Financial Performance
Your history of producing revenue and profit combined with the professionalism of your record keeping.

Growth Potential
Your likelihood to grow your business in the future and at what rate.

Switzerland Structure
How dependent your business is on any one employee, customer or supplier.

Valuation Teeter Totter
Whether your business is a cash suck or a cash spigot.

Recurring Revenue
The proportion and quality of automatic, annuity-based revenue you collect each month.

Monopoly Control
How well differentiated your business is from competitors in your industry.

Customer Satisfaction
The likelihood that your customers will re-purchase and also refer you.

Hub & Spoke
How your business would perform if you were unexpectedly unable to work for a period of three months.

The **Value**Builder System™

Dependence—The Switzerland Structure

Is the business overly dependent on any one customer, employee, or supplier? If so, this negatively impacts its value because buyers are concerned about the real risk of that loss.

The opposite of this is a business that isn't dependent on any one customer, employee, or supplier. There's little to no risk if a single customer is lost. There's also minimal risk with a business that has a strong training process and can quickly replace any employee. The same is true of a business that can source material at comparable prices from a wide variety of suppliers. In each of these instances, a business that experiences little to no impact from a change in customer, employee, or supplier is much more stable and less risky than a business dependent on one or more of these factors.

Valuation Teeter-Totter

This measures the impact of cash flow, gross margin, and profitability on the value of a business. It refers to the relationship between working capital and earnings. If your working capital grows out of proportion to the cash generated by the business, then a buyer won't be willing to pay more for the earnings because they'll need to write an additional (and potentially bigger) check for the working capital. If a business generates cash as it grows and requires little additional working capital because the business funds its own expansion, then a buyer is likely to pay more for the earnings.

Recurring Revenue

How is the sales revenue generated? This is one of the primary areas of interest for a buyer. If a business has a high degree of recurring customers or a business model that relies on regular, recurring subscription-type payments from its customers, then it's easy for a buyer to value the future stream of revenue. If a business must go out and hunt new customers month after month and has little or no recurring revenue from its existing customers, then its future stream of revenue is harder to value and has a higher risk associated with it. High risk always leads to a discount in value. Highly reliable revenue streams lead to low risk and an increase in value.

Monopoly Control

This dimension of value measures the uniqueness of a business. A unique business is difficult for competitors to duplicate and, therefore, earns a premium measure in this area. If a business is commoditized and easily duplicated in the marketplace, then the business value is reduced. This differentiation from the competition makes a particular business opportunity unique and meaningful. Strategic buyers often seek out these types of businesses for acquisition.

Customer Satisfaction

This dimension measures both the extent to which customers are satisfied as well as a business's ability to assess customer satisfaction in a consistent and rigorous way. Satisfied customers often equate to loyal customers, and loyal customers deliver referrals and recurring revenue. A business that proactively measures customer satisfaction and can demonstrate it has a system and process of growing satisfaction over time is often more valuable to a buyer than a comparable business with no measurement or control system.

Hub & Spoke

This measures how dependent the business is on the owner's efforts within it. If the owner is the center of all functions, the business will enter a phase of high risk when the owner steps away. On the other hand, if a business is able to succeed and grow with little to no impact from the owner's absence, then the business risk is low for a potential buyer. Many buyers fear what impact an ownership change will have on a business. If the impact is little to none, then a buyer will place a higher value on the business.

HOW DO I DETERMINE THE VALUE THAT FAIRLY REPRESENTS MY BUSINESS?

Determining value is a matter of informed judgment. In an actual buy-sell transaction, the sale price is based on the value the buyer and seller have perceived, plus their negotiating skills and the pressure on each side to buy or sell. This type of transaction normally represents an *arm's length* transaction, where value is ultimately agreed upon between buyer and seller. When you equip yourself with a thorough analysis of the financial and operational dimensions described herein, you're in a much better position to achieve the highest valuation possible for your business. You're also in a strong position to communicate the data, which enables a buyer to effectively measure the risk in many dimensions of the business performance. This helps assure the buyer that they're receiving good value for the price even when the price is higher than they hoped to pay.

When you equip yourself with a thorough analysis of the financial and operational dimensions described herein, you're in a much better position to achieve the highest valuation possible for your business.

At the advice of the consultant, Bill hired a professional broker. He'd discovered another path—one that he'd been unaware of—and he and his broker got to work. They set a timeline and called in reinforcements to help mitigate some of the business pressures. Finally, things were beginning to turn around for Bill.

He was happy to learn that his broker was working on a valuation that was likely to dictate an asking price greater than what Bill had expected—even greater than he had told the few buyers he'd already engaged. This was comforting news, and he was holding his breath in anticipation of it being confirmed.

He was also very busy renegotiating his existing agreements. He was kicking himself that he'd let them become so out of date and was beginning to see what a huge roadblock he could avoid thanks to his broker's diligence.

Mark was also busy compiling information in preparation for due diligence. He was excited to see offers coming in, and as his team had led him to expect, the range of offers varied widely. The team set the expectation that the offer amounts would be similar by buyer types, and they definitely were seeing that pattern emerge.

CHAPTER
8

HOW TO MARKET THE BUSINESS

The marketing process had reached its allotted end, and Mark's broker called a meeting to evaluate all the offers they'd received. The offers fell into three ranges—low, medium, and high—compared to what they'd expected. They decided the best course of action was to go back to the buyers with the top five offers and tell them they were in the final group. They would have one last opportunity to modify their bids. The team set a two-week deadline and issued the notifications.

As expected, this created a frenzy of activity. The top five players all requested additional information. Many also wanted to understand specifically where they stood and what it would take to win. The broker kept all parties on an even playing field and was careful to ensure that everyone had the same information. If one party asked for something that nobody else had requested, they updated the FAQ document and shared it with everyone.

As for Bill, he was now busy putting together the appropriate information his broker had requested. Much of the data wasn't convenient, so Bill had to dig through his business records to find it. He and his broker agreed they needed a buyer who was familiar and experienced with Bill's business type, had the financial resources to move quickly, and was interested in a turn-around opportunity. This limited the field of potential buyers, but it did give them a clear vision of their ideal buyer.

THE IDEAL BUYER

In 1989, the late author, educator, and businessman, Steven Covey, introduced the phrase "Begin with the end in mind." Business opportunity marketing plans should be developed using this mantra. It's an excellent way to begin to identify the ideal buyer.

For many sellers, the ideal buyer is the person or entity that will take the least amount of time in diligence, is prepared to pay the highest price in cash at closing, and won't change a thing concerning the business operation. An ideal buyer is rare and highly sought after.

An ideal buyer is rare and highly sought after.

When it comes to identifying the ideal buyer, several attributes are clearly recognizable. First is their ability to pay the asking price. It's normal and customary for potential buyers to exhibit their ability to pay either through their own resources or by demonstrating their borrowing capacity. Brokers and advisors will have a process in place where prospective buyers qualify themselves.

Another clearly recognizable attribute is industry experience or relevance. This is particularly important if a portion of the purchase price will be financed. Lenders look long and hard at experience when they qualify a buyer for lending. If SBA funding is contemplated, this attribute is required.

TARGET IDEAL BUYER MOTIVATION

The marketing message needs to speak to the motivation of the ideal buyer. The buyer seeks a certain something, so the seller's message should speak to that certain something. This core message should be part of all marketing elements.

The marketing elements include the headlines used in the advertising methods. A headline should shout to the ideal buyer and herald a single key feature of the opportunity. It should stop the buyer and get them to investigate further, to seek the additional detail.

The additional detail is referred to as *teaser data*. It should include up to five key benefits the opportunity represents and also provide some basic financial information like annual gross revenue and some measurement of profit and cash flow. This allows the browsing buyer to quickly identify if the opportunity fits their criteria.

At that point, the prospective buyer may request additional information, which opens the door for you to learn about the buyer.

RESPONSE TIME

Imagine you're a buyer seeking a strategic tuck-in acquisition to broaden your product line or geographic reach. Often buyers will subscribe to business-for-sale websites and are alerted when a business that fits your criteria is available. You might also send inquiries to business brokers, advisors, lenders, attorneys, and valuation specialists within your target markets and ask to be alerted when opportunities present themselves. As a buyer, you're motivated to do a deal and are looking for something specific, so you fish in as many ponds as possible to find the perfect catch.

Then you get a lead. An alert pops up or an email arrives from one of the specialists you contacted. You immediately seek more information because you want to know if this is the opportunity you desire. And then all you hear is crickets. The seller takes an inordinate amount of time to respond.

Does this really happen? Unfortunately, surveys of buyers report that sixty to seventy percent of the time, they don't receive a timely response.

Why not?

For DIY sellers, it's often a matter of priority. They're busy running their company, so the additional burden and responsibility of managing a sale process comes second to the day-to-day responsibilities of running the business. Or sometimes the seller's email server flags the incoming message as being from an unknown sender and moves the message into a spam folder. For a whole variety of reasons, sellers often don't respond immediately, so buyers move on to another opportunity.

> *Often when a DIY seller gets an inquiry and responds in a reasonable time period, they respond in a way that doesn't honor the buyer.*

Often when a DIY seller gets an inquiry and responds in a reasonable time period, they respond in a way that doesn't honor the buyer. The seller may ask for a lot of information from the buyer in an attempt to qualify them to learn more. Or if the buyer is a competitor, the seller won't want to provide them with the specific information they need to qualify the opportunity. There are many different ways a DIY seller can kill a deal before it has a chance to get started.

To keep the process moving forward, here are some practices to engage as many potential buyers as possible:

1. Respond to inquiries in a timely fashion (the same day if possible).

2. Provide a brief synopsis of the opportunity to allow the buyer to determine quickly if the opportunity fits their profile.

3. Make the exchange of information easy. For example, if you require confidentiality agreements, have them prepared and ready to share.

4. Honor the buyer's inquiry and operate from a perspective of gratitude with a sincere desire to try and find an ideal fit.

IS IT NECESSARY FOR BUYERS TO WALK THROUGH THE BUSINESS?

Your employees, customers, and suppliers probably don't know your business is being marketed for sale. You may feel that if you let buyers walk through the business during normal business hours, it would put your business in jeopardy. But buyers want to see the business operating. They want to see how it performs in its normal course of action and to get a sense of how it's received by its customers and market.

How do you resolve this?

As mentioned earlier, consider producing a pictorial of your business. Hire a professional real estate photographer to come out and take photos. This allows you to show the buyer a comprehensive view of the business without the buyer being physically present. You can arrange the photo shoot to minimize the impact on business operations.

Photos achieve two key goals:

- They give the buyer a visual image of the business that satisfies their initial curiosity and ensures the business fits their criteria.
- They enable you to have minimal disruption to your business operations during the sale process.

There will come a time when the buyer wants to visit the business before the sale is completed. But a wise seller won't want that to happen until well after the diligence process has begun. The site visit becomes a confirmation visit during the diligence process, not an interruption of your daily business operations. During the diligence stage, there may be several different types of inspections and visits that occur, and you'll have time to coordinate them appropriately.

Mark was quite proud of the marketing documents his team had assembled. In fact, he'd been integral to the creation of the CIM. Due to the nature and complexity of Mark's business, the document and its attachments numbered almost two hundred pages. Mark had his hand in the creation of every page, which he enjoyed immensely. The images and illustrations were a particular point of pride for him. He felt they showed off his life's work in a very favorable light. He shared the CIM with his family and a few peers who also owned businesses, and he kept a copy in his briefcase in case any other opportunity came up for him to share it.

Bill was still a little overwhelmed with the whole process. He was struggling to pull together the required information, but he was making some progress. He hadn't realized how much was involved in putting together a comprehensive marketing package. The financial information and representations really surprised him. His bookkeeper produced the operating reports each month, and they typically ran about twenty pages. Bill was amazed his broker reduced those to three concise pages that were much easier to understand than the reports he he'd poured through for the last twenty-five years. He was beginning to understand why he'd been so frustrated by trying to sell his business alone and how having an experienced broker was already benefitting him.

HOW TO NEGOTIATE
THE SALE PRICE

Mark and his team had received five final offers at the top end of their range, and they were busy answering questions and analyzing them. They settled on a strategy that best suited Mark's needs and would minimize his tax impact, so he would receive the largest potential net proceeds. Most of the offers contained some or most of the terms desired, and the team was confident they could achieve their objectives.

Bill was working with his broker to finalize the marketing package. He was quite impressed with the price rationale portion of the package. His broker provided a pretty compelling argument, and while he cautioned Bill not to expect the full amount they were asking for, Bill was quite pleased the price range would allow him to meet all his outstanding financial obligations and then some. He felt hopeful this process would get him out of troubled waters.

ASKING PRICE

The initial assessment and valuation will establish the current fair market range of your business. From this range, an asking price is determined. It's important to start with this target price because, from a negotiation standpoint, the asking price frames the resulting discussions and negotiations.

> *The initial assessment and valuation will establish the current fair market range of your business. From this range, an asking price is determined.*

Of course, the asking price should always be the realistic top end of the range you'd expect to get for your business. You want to establish the best you hope for within the current fair market range. Every business has strengths and weaknesses, and different buyers may attribute different values to those strengths and weaknesses. So, begin at the top of the range and leave room to negotiate down and still be satisfied with the result.

The evaluation and assessment enable you to quantify your rationale for setting the asking price. When it's a reasonable calculation using specific data points, it's easy to respond when a buyer asks, "How did you arrive at that price?" You (or your representative) can then discuss how you arrived at that price.

Buyers will ask that question, particularly when dealing with a DIY seller, because they know that DIY sellers often don't have a relevant formula for determining their price. More often than not, a DIY seller uses an outdated formula or makes an emotional assessment of what the business is worth to him or her. This gives the buyer an advantage because they almost always do their homework, and they're familiar with current fair market values.

SELLERS EQUATION

Price
Terms
Costs
Taxes

Variables
During
Negotiation

Net Proceeds

Price + Terms - Costs - Taxes = Net Proceeds

What matters MOST is
what the Seller gets to
KEEP after the
transition if complete

INNOVATIVE
Coaching · Valuation · Brokerage

> *More often than not, a DIY seller uses an*
> *outdated formula or makes an emotional*
> *assessment of what the business is worth*
> *to him or her.*

Professional brokers and mergers and acquisitions (M/A) advisors have access to various database tools that provide data on comparable transactions. There are a number of professional associations that voluntarily collect private business transaction specifics exactly for the purpose of providing comps. This data is generated from mergers and acquisition professionals, lenders, and other affiliated professional organizations. With a professional broker involved, this data provides another level of detail when establishing a price and then defending that price during negotiation.

EMOTIONAL ISSUES

As the seller, you're certainly emotionally invested in your business, which can sometimes cloud your thinking. You know how the business operates and can see all the opportunities for improvement that you assume the new buyer will develop. You feel like you've done all of the heavy lifting of establishing the company, and the buyer will have nothing but blue skies in front of them. This causes you to be inflexible in your price, which becomes a liability during the negotiation process. Professional advising can help you avoid a pitfall like this.

Guess what? Buyers aren't emotional. They look at the past performance as indication of future performance and assume that you've taken advantage of every opportunity that presented itself in the past. A buyer's mindset is based on a rational approach of accepting past performance and attempting to apply a discount in order to give them some room for error in the future. DIY sellers are rarely prepared for this and might view a buyer's discounted offer as a personal offense.

However, buyers will sometimes make a ridiculous low-ball offer to see how much room there is for negotiation. For an inexperienced DIY seller, their initial response is to be incredibly offended. Emotions take the upper hand, and they may even shut down all communication from that point forward.

Savvy buyers are on the lookout for this type of response. They know if they can set the seller off at will, it gives them a negotiating advantage. Any time they need to (in order to gain an advantage), they can make some form of unreasonable request and send the seller off into an emotional tailspin.

Savvy buyers have a wide range of tactics in their arsenal to gain an advantage over sellers. Sending a DIY seller to compete against a savvy buyer is like sending a child to compete against a college athlete—the odds are not in the child's favor. Savvy buyers know this and use their advantage to employ an old adage: you get what you negotiate.

> *Sending a DIY seller to compete against a savvy buyer is like sending a child to compete against a college athlete—the odds are not in the child's favor.*

This is yet another instance where brokers and advisors are useful. They advocate on your behalf. They're professional players and know all the tactics and techniques; they prepare for these approaches and build their arsenal to defend their position. They may even take advantage of these approaches as they occur. Brokers and advisors benefit when you benefit, so they play hard to achieve the best outcome.

OFFERS FOR MORE THAN ASKING PRICE

Is it possible to get an offer for more than asking price? Yes! And it can even be engineered to occur. The best way to get more than asking price is to get multiple buyers to bid against each other simultaneously. Professional brokers can engineer this situation, which often leads to offers over asking price. It doesn't always happen, but the goal is to create a greater level of demand than supply.

When multiple buyers are engaged, they bid against each other. It's very similar to how platforms like eBay work—an auction process drives up prices, and it's a reliable way to maximize your selling price.

To create a bidding war, you need two very interested buyers. Ideally, it's better to have more than two buyers who have all agreed to confidentiality and have received various informational documents. To achieve the maximum benefit, you must tell all the buyers that there are other buyers engaged and let them know if their offer isn't in a lead position. Many times, they'll be willing to improve their initial offer.

A word of caution: some buyers will flat-out refuse to participate in a bidding war because they know the net result is to increase the sale price or because of confidentiality concerns. That's okay as long as you have others that are willing to play.

HOW TO COUNTER AN OFFER

Hopefully there's more than one buyer involved and the asking price established a starting point in your discussions. The buyer reviewed all of the supplied information from your marketing package and may have sought additional details. This opportunity fits the buyer's criteria, and they're very similar to your ideal buyer. It's time for them to present their offer.

The offer should be presented in writing and come in one of these various forms:

1. Indication of Interest
2. Letter of Intent
3. Offer to Purchase
4. Negotiated Term Sheet

While they are slightly different in format, all are formal offers and should be taken seriously. These specific elements should be included:

- What is the form of transaction? Share sale or asset purchase?
- What is the total purchase price?
- How will the price be conveyed? In total at closing, in installments, or another option?
- Will financing be required?
- Is the buyer providing earnest money?
- Is the buyer asking for exclusivity?
- What is the time period for due diligence?
- When and where will the closing take place?
- Is the offer dependent on any contingencies?
- What is the role/responsibilities of the seller after closing?
- What are the terms of the non-compete?

Many other elements may be included, and each of the above could contain several particular clauses. In general, both the buyer and seller are best served when the offer document contains all the pertinent business issues regarding the transaction.

Let's assume the buyer offered you a different amount than you were seeking. How should you respond? The best way is with gratitude for their interest. And then you can ask questions designed to understand how they constructed their offer. If you want to understand the buyer's financial formula, then you can enter into a productive discussion regarding the difference between your rationale for the asking price and their rationale for the offer price.

There can be valid reasons for differences in price. If there's a good fit between the buyer and you, the two parties can usually find a solution where you each meet your needs and protect your interests. This isn't easy, but when both parties have a clear understanding of each other's objectives and valuation methodologies, solutions can be found.

Let's assume the buyer offered you a different amount than you were seeking. How should you respond? The best way is with gratitude for their interest.

Remember that the price is one thing—the terms are another. It may be to your advantage to consider a lower up-front price, coupled with a consulting agreement and a potential future bonus as a way to bridge the gap between what you want and what's been offered.

Again, having a team on your side helps. Someone on your team may have experience with a structure that neither the seller or the buyer has considered. At the end of the day, the key factors in a deal that benefits both parties always include a willing and able buyer that works with a willing and able seller.

Mark and his team scheduled video calls with each of the potential buyers. They shared their preferred vision and structure for the transaction and left the price and some of the financial terms up to the buyers. One potential buyer dropped out at that stage, but Mark still had four buyers who clearly conveyed their desire to honor his preferred terms. A final date was established for each of the four contenders to deliver their final offers, and they all made adjustments to their original terms and met the date. At the end of the day, one offer stood above the rest, and Mark's team scheduled another video call with the winning buyer to finalize the terms of the Letter of Intent.

After the Letter of Intent was negotiated and signed, Mark's broker notified each of the other finalists that a deal was pending. He told them they'd be kept informed during the diligence period so that if the deal fell apart, they could be ready to act. This kept the other three potential buyers engaged up to the day of closing.

Meanwhile, Bill's price was set, and the initial marketing process had begun. He didn't know about the competitors in his market and was pleased to get a quick indication of interest from one of them. His broker cautioned him not to get too excited, but he was beginning to breathe a sigh of relief that someone was genuinely interested in his business. He was surprised at the amount of clarification the buyer requested and was happy his broker was extremely discreet with the information shared. They hadn't committed anything to writing yet, but Bill could feel this was getting serious quickly.

WHAT IS DUE DILIGENCE?

By the time you get to this point, you and the buyer have agreed on the primary economic terms of the sale. The price, terms, and timing are set, and both parties will develop a purchase agreement, which ultimately transfers ownership of the business.

This is also the time when your roles reverse. Up to this point, you've generated information and documents for the buyer. Now the buyer comes to you requesting specific information they need in order to finalize the transaction.

A sample diligence document request checklist is shown below. While not applicable to all transactions, it will give you a sense of the breadth and depth of the information that buyers normally request. It's your responsibility to provide the information desired.

DUE DILIGENCE CHECKLIST

Corporate Records and Organization:
- The current charter documents

Financings:
- Schedule of all short-term and long-term debt, including capitalized leases, guarantees, and other contingent obligations

- All documents and agreements evidencing borrowings or available borrowings, whether secured or unsecured, including indentures, loan and credit agreements, promissory notes, letter of credit reimbursement agreements, and other evidence of indebtedness and guarantees
- All documents and agreements evidencing other financing arrangements, including sale and lease-back arrangements and installment purchases

Assets:

- List of real property owned by the business together with its location, description of all encumbrances, and a brief description of the property and its uses
- List and copies of real property leases and subleases owned by the business and all relating correspondence
- Copies of all deeds, title insurance policies or title insurance commitments, and surveys of all real property owned by the business and copies of all engineering or architectural plans prepared with respect to it
- Copies of any outstanding notices of violations or similar notices received from any governmental authority or insurance company related to the use, operation, or maintenance of any real property owned or leased by the business
- Copies of all contracts of option agreements for the acquisition of real property by the business
- List of personal property owned, including property in the hands of third parties, such as machinery, furniture, furnishings, computers, equipment, etc., including cost, accumulated depreciation, and net book value
- All agreements encumbering real or personal property owned by the business or any of its

subsidiaries, including mortgages, deeds of trust, and security agreements
- Copies of certificates of title to all vehicles of the business
- Documents relating to any material write-down or write-off of any asset over the past three years

Other Agreements:
- All joint ventures and partnership agreements
- All licensing agreements, franchises, and conditional sales contracts
- Copies of service warranties, if any, held or issued by the business
- All collective bargaining agreements, employment agreements, and consulting agreements
- All documents, including indemnity agreements, relating to any acquisitions or dispositions by the business and any merger, consolidation, or other combination of the business with any other entity
- All sales agency and manufacturer representative agreements
- Any agreements with any supplier, which has accounted for more than 5 percent of total purchases in either of the last two fiscal years
- Any agreements with any customer, which has accounted for more than 5 percent of sales in either of the last two fiscal years
- Any agreements with any supplier who is the sole source of supply for any essential products
- Any agreements with any customer, which is the sole source of sales for any products
- The business's standard terms of sale and any warranties given but not included in standard terms of sale
- The business's standard terms of purchase and any warranties received but not included in the standard terms of purchase

- All documents relating to any other transactions between the business and any director, officer, or owner or more than 5 percent of the stock of the business
- All documents pertaining to any receivables from or payables to directors, officers, or owners of more than 5 percent of the stock of the business
- All forms of contracts typically entered into between the business and its customers or suppliers in the ordinary course

Intangibles:

- A schedule of all patents, trademarks, copyrights, service marks and applications therefore, and software used in the business or that relate to the business name, indicating those owned, subject to adverse claims, and jurisdictions in which registered
- List of patents, trademarks, copyrights, service marks and applications therefore, and software used in the business or which relate to the business name that are not owned (and any related claims or litigation), and identify owner of such information and provide license or other royalty agreements
- Description of non-patented proprietary information
- Confidentiality and non-disclosure agreements
- Description of any interference, infringement, or unfair competition matters, whether current or potential
- All correspondence between the business and any federal or state agency or other third party relating to any of the items set forth
- All royalty and license agreements involving the business
- All contracts or agreements that obligate the business to indemnify a third party
- All contracts or agreements for the future purchase of, or payment for, supplies, products, or services

- All contracts or agreements to sell or supply products or to perform services
- All contracts or agreements (current or proposed) limiting or restraining the business from engaging in or competing in any lines of business, or locations, with any person, firm, corporation, or other entity
- A description of all oral contracts, agreements, or commitments of the business
- List of all agents, suppliers, customers, and distributors of the business
- List of all agreements under which the other party would have the right to terminate upon or following the proposed transaction or the consummation of the proposed transaction would constitute a breach or default by business
- Any agreements involving payments in excess of $10,000 or involving payments based on profits or sales
- All other contracts, agreements, or commitments that are material to the operations of the business or that may have a material effect on the business or their respective assets, properties, business operations, or financial condition
- Any surety and performance bonds
- Any consulting agreements
- Any confidentiality or non-competition agreements
- Any government contracts or subcontracts
- Any research and development agreements
- Any indemnification agreements with officers, directors, and others
- Any material agreements not previously described or currently being negotiated
- Any corporate manuals outlining internal policies or procedures
- Any agreements relating to computer hardware or software
- Any maintenance agreements

- Correspondence relating to any disputes under contracts, including actual, threatened, and potential breaches

Environmental and Related Matters:

- All internal business reports or reports prepared by third parties and furnished to the business concerning environmental matters relating to business properties
- Copies of any statements or reports given to the Federal Environmental Protection Agency or any state department of environmental regulation or any similar state or local regulatory body, authority, or agency
- All notices, complaints, suits, orders, or similar documents sent to, received by, or served upon the business by the Federal Environmental Protection Agency or any state or local department of environmental regulation or any similar state or local regulatory body, authority, or agency
- All business or outside reports concerning compliance with waste disposal regulations (hazardous or otherwise)
- A list of all hazardous materials, hazardous substances, or hazardous wastes used or generated at any of the business' facilities, including Material Safety Data Sheets
- Copies of all environmental investigations, reviews or assessments, including without limitation phase I and phase II environmental assessments, with respect to real property (whether owned or leased) of the business
- Copies of all written complaints from employees, neighbors, or members of the general public concerning environmental compliance violations, property damage, or personal injury allegedly resulting from the release or presence of hazardous substances or wastes on or from facility currently or previously owned or

leased by the business, together with a description of the resolution or status of each such complaint

Personnel and Labor Matters:

- Organizational charts and list of all employees including starting date, position, salary, and benefits
- Documents (including summary plan descriptions) representing any bonus, retirement, profit sharing, incentive compensation, pension, and other employee benefit plans or agreements, and any correspondence relating thereto with beneficiaries thereof or any regulators
- Schedule of all restricted stock, options and SARs, indicating whether any stock options are incentive or non-qualified stock options, exercise price, when exercisable and other terms
- Documents and correspondence representing or relating to workers compensation or disability policies and any claims with respect thereto
- All liability insurance policies for employees, directors, and officers
- Annual reports and IRS Form 5500s for pension plans and welfare plans. For each tax-qualified employee benefit plan:
- Plan and trust document
- Summary plan description
- Last three years of IRS annual reports (form 5500)
- Last three years of IRS determination letters
- Last three years of actuarial valuations
- Copies of all determination letters issued by the IRS with respect to any employee benefit plans and copies of all pending requests for determination letters
- Copies (and, if oral, written summaries) of all personnel policy manuals and all other personnel policies and all current employee handbooks and/or work rules

- Samples of all employment application forms
- A list of all pending or threatened complaints, claims, charges, or investigations (and those that have occurred in the past five years) against the business or any officer, director, employee, or agent of the business, pursuant to the Equal Pay Act, the Wage and Hour Act, or any other federal, state, or local statute or regulation dealing with employment
- List of all pending or threatened (and those that have occurred within the past five years) unfair labor practice claims, equal employment opportunity discrimination complaints, charges or investigations, or any other employee claims or charges filed with any government or court
- List and brief description of any labor relation problems, work stoppages, or strikes that have occurred in the past five years
- Summary plan descriptions for each of the business's welfare benefit plans like life, medical, disability, and others

Tax and Financial Matters:
- List state, local, and foreign income, franchise, property, real estate, unemployment, sales/use and other taxes to which the business is subject, assets or income of the business, as follows:
- Government assessment date, return filing date, tax due date
- All federal, state, and local (including foreign) tax returns filed for the past three years.
- All correspondence with the Internal Revenue Service or state or local tax authorities concerning adjustments or questioning compliance
- Any agreements, consents, elections, or waivers filed or made by the corporation with any taxing authority

- List of returns and the years thereof that have been audited by federal, state, or local tax authorities and copies of determination letters related thereto
- List and description of all pending or threatened disputes with regard to tax matters involving the business
- Correspondence with the business's accountants prepared or received during the past three years, including all management letters from the accountants
- Representation letters to auditors for the last three years
- Brief description of any change in accounting policies or procedures during the past five years

Litigation, Government, and Regulatory Issues:
- A list and brief description of all suits, actions, litigation, arbitrations, claims, and administrative proceedings or other governmental investigations or inquiries, pending or threatened or commenced (whether or not concluded) by or against the business in the past three years
- A list of, and settlement agreements for, all litigation, arbitration, and claims settled or concluded within the past three years
- All correspondence with, reports of or to, filings with, or other information with respect to any other regulatory bodies, which regulate any portion of the business within the past three years
- All reports, notices, or correspondence relating to any alleged violation or infringement by the business of, or otherwise relating to the status of the business's compliance with, any local, state, or federal law of governmental regulations, orders, or permits within the past three years
- Copies of all inspections or other reports issued by any governmental authorities with respect to the business

- A schedule detailing the number of customer complaints (including product liability claims or complaints) received by the business, including an analysis of such complaints and the appropriate resolutions and related costs
- All licenses, permits, and governmental authorizations held or required to be held by the business
- All regulatory reports (domestic or foreign) required to be filed during any of the past three years

Miscellaneous:

- A schedule of all insurance policies and self-insurance programs, including detail on premiums, insurer, coverage, and deductibles
- Copies of existing insurance policies, including property damage, third party liability, products liability, group health insurance, D&O, and key employee
- List of products and services currently sold by the business, together with applicable prices and discounts
- List of the ten largest suppliers, showing percentage of total purchases from each supplier
- Any other documents or information that are significant with respect to any portion of the business or that should be considered and reviewed in making disclosures regarding the business and its financial condition to prospective investors

This is a daunting list for a DIY seller. And since they haven't been involved in a transaction before, they likely won't expect to receive such a comprehensive list.

This is a daunting list for a DIY seller. And since they haven't been involved in a transaction before, they likely won't expect to receive such a comprehensive list. When the buyer presents the list of required documents for the due diligence period, the process of locating, copying, conveying, and then addressing any issues within the documents can overwhelm the seller. This is one of the reasons the majority of transactions entered into by DIY sellers never reach closing.

Meanwhile, a professionally managed team prepares for this request from the beginning. Your broker or advisors will ask you to gather this information while your business is being marketed. This gives you time to locate, review, and take care of any particular issues with the documents. Then when it's time to share them with the buyer, they're already organized and reflect the present state of the business.

Mark spent the majority of his time during the marketing period assembling the records for due diligence and uploading them to the data vault. It gave him something productive to do. His team reviewed each document and found many small changes that were necessary to make the transfer happen. This enabled Mark to engage with the opposing party on a casual basis to update the files, and he was grateful not to have any pressure on him to meet a buyer-imposed deadline.

Bill had a lot of work to do. His records weren't in good shape, and it became almost a full-time job to get them in order. He was thankful for the guidance of his advisor and couldn't help but wonder what might have happened if he hadn't had the oversight to get this done ahead of time.

TRANSITIONING THE BUSINESS TO THE BUYER

The closing will come, and all the documents must be signed. A mountain of paper will sit in front of both you and the buyer, and the review and actual signature process will probably take longer than you expect. But soon it will all be done!

The completed document list may look like this:

1. Asset Purchase Agreement or Share Purchase Agreement
2. Bill of Sale
3. Disclosure Statements
4. FFE Listing Detail
5. Allocation of Purchase Price
6. Non-Compete Agreement
7. Training / Consulting Agreement
8. Notices for Creditors / Suppliers / Customers
9. Tax Clearance
10. Financing Agreements

The due diligence period gives the buyer all the facts. Now, the seller must give them all the details.

The deal closed on a Friday. Mark was in the office the next Monday, as early as always. He turned off the office alarm and turned on the coffee maker, just like he'd done every other morning for the last thirty years. But it felt different. He was glad he'd had the weekend to think about his new role. The new owner would be arriving soon, and later that morning, they'd call in all their outside people for a meeting. Mark was a little nervous about it, but he knew they were prepared.

The new owner arrived at the appointed time, and Mark escorted him to his office. Mark offered him the desk, but the new owner graciously declined—that was Mark's place. They closed the door and reviewed the agenda for the upcoming meeting.

Mark was really impressed by both the attention to detail and genuine concern the new owner had for how the staff would react to the change. He was definitely doing everything necessary to assure everyone that this was a new chapter in the business history, but they would proceed according to the strategic plan already established.

The meeting went well. Many said that they'd known the day was coming, since Mark wasn't getting any younger. Everybody seemed impressed with the level of candor and information the new owner provided. The fact the he knew everyone's names and responsibilities impressed them.

The new owner assured them that their jobs wouldn't change. In fact, he stressed how he needed them now more than ever. He and Mark both talked about how Mark would be there every day for the next few months and then would take an extended vacation. After that, Mark would come in a couple of times a week over the next six months.

There were a few questions. They wanted to know if their checks would come out on the same days and if the benefit package would change. Overall, the staff seemed to take the news as well as one could hope. The meeting ended on a very positive note, and the day progressed like any other Monday.

Bill's experience was a little different. His sales transaction had been an asset purchase, which meant that there were many changes that would affect the business. Bill agreed to stay for six months to help with the transition. It was going to be an intense amount of work.

For starters, the buyer formed a new corporation, which meant all suppliers and employees would be working for a new entity. All their agreements had to be renegotiated, and Bill had to keep his corporation open to settle all accounts. There were a few tense moments, but eventually all major suppliers agreed to comparable terms.

It was a little different for the employees. Bill had kept more staff than the current business volume justified, so several employees were let go. Bill was responsible to fund their severance, and thankfully he now had the funds to do so. The new company had a different payroll system that changed the pay dates, but the owner agreed to honor existing pay rates for the employees that remained. The benefits program was different but very similar in range. Most received this change well, but some did not.

To Bill's surprise, the new owner negotiated a much more favorable term on the lease. Bill was initially upset about that. He'd been a good tenant for more than two decades and was surprised that the landlord agreed to charge the new owner a lower rate.

Bill's lease had annual escalators, and he'd never taken the time to see if his increased rate was competitive in the current market.

In fact, Bill was also surprised to learn the new owner had gotten better insurance rates and better service contract rates. In fact, the new owner was much more adept at managing working capital, which meant that they'd begin operating on day one with significantly less cost than Bill had on his final day of ownership. He was initially resentful but quickly realized that he could've enjoyed the same benefit if he'd focused on the same things.

On the night before the closing, Bill and the new owner jointly performed an inventory after business hours. When they came to agreement on the total value, Bill was surprised when the new owner cleaned out the storeroom and discarded what Bill thought was perfectly salable merchandise. But that was the new owner's prerogative; he now owned it.

Bill's employment agreement stated his salary, which was slightly less than a competitive market rate, and a clear set of duties and responsibilities. He was still the general manager, but he was, of course, no longer the owner. He quickly learned what it meant to have a boss. The new owner met with Bill at the same time every week to review his performance. They reviewed the key performance indicators of the business and discussed where to put their attention to deliver the desired outcome. It became quite clear to the new owner that there were some employees who weren't pulling their weight. Bill agreed, but he'd been much more tolerant in the past. He quickly found out that those tolerant days were over.

The six-month employment period went by

quickly. While Bill initially was resentful of the lower cost and tighter standards, he came to see that it was healthy for the business. In fact, the business was performing much better than it had in years. Bill was proud to have a hand in that.

KEY TAKEAWAYS

Selling a business involves negotiating many terms, including the terms of your exit. Buyers often want you to stay involved for a period of time to help them come to grips with all the vagaries of the business. It actually benefits all parties—you get time to say goodbye to the business you built, and if there's an earn-out or seller note involved, this time period allows you to have an impact on those areas.

> *Selling a business involves negotiating many terms, including the terms of your exit. Buyers often want you to stay involved for a period of time to help them come to grips with all the vagaries of the business.*

The buyer can't possibly learn everything there is to know about your business during the diligence period, so having you around after the sale gives them a coach and confidant. And for the customers and employees, having you and the buyer work together in the business provides a level of continuity and stability. The entire business benefits.

It'll be hard for you to no longer be the authority. This is a new position, and you have to learn the boundaries. You won't like all the decisions the new owner makes. But the new owner is now the authority, and their decisions stand.

The proceeds from the sale and the prospect of a new phase of life will comfort you during this transition period. Then you can watch with pride while the new owner takes the business to new heights.

A NEW DAY

The morning sun broke over the ocean, promising another warm, beautiful day to Mark and his wife. They'd always dreamed of spending the winter on the beach, and they were now enjoying every minute of it. The timing had been perfect—a closing on the last day of their fiscal year, a couple months of transition services to the new buyer, and now they were booked for four months at a world-class resort on the beach.

Their plan was to take a little time to themselves and then spend some time with the kids and grandkids. After a summer trip with the grandkids, they wanted to set up a business entrepreneurship program for aspiring start-ups, so they could mentor young entrepreneurs. They were truly living the American dream.

Bill and his wife were also celebrating. They'd received just enough money to pay back all the business loans and, incredibly, put a couple of hundred thousand dollars toward their savings. While Bill would need to go back to work, he no longer had the constant worry that had haunted him for the last year. In fact, he was looking forward to finding new work. He'd invested twenty-five years in his business, and now his non-compete kept him from working in the same industry, but he was ready and excited for a change. The last several years had been grueling, and he was anxious for the day when he could leave work and not take it home with him.

But Bill wasn't sure what he would do. So, his broker put together an inventory of his skills. Once he saw them written on paper, Bill was proud of the wide range of skills he had to offer. He was confident that many industries could use his talents, and his savings allowed him to take his time to find the right fit.

Bill's only regret, if pressed to discuss it, was that he'd waited too long to ask for help. After getting professional help and going through an orchestrated process, he was surprised by how quickly it had all come together. Sure, it was a lot of work, and what he hadn't known had certainly cost him and his family time and money. But he was thankful to be on the other side without any personal guarantees hanging over him.

ABOUT THE AUTHOR

STEVEN DENNY is a partner with Innovative Business Advisors, a mergers and acquisitions firm specializing in serving companies of $1 million to $50 million in enterprise value. The firm provides M/A services, business valuation services, exit planning, and specialized coaching services designed to help business owners grow enterprise value and profits.

Steve began his career in business development with a Fortune 100 firm and was one of the youngest vice presidents in his industry. He eventually attained a senior executive role with national responsibilities. After twenty-five years of service in the industry, he retired and founded ABN, a business consulting and brokerage business in Saint Louis, Missouri in 2005. In 2018, Steve merged his firm with Innovative Business Advisors and was recognized as one of "The Best M&A Providers in Saint Louis."

Steve and his wife Debi reside in suburban Saint Louis and enjoy spending time with their children and grandchildren.

How to connect with Steve:
Web: www.innovativeba.com
Email: Steve@innovativeba.com
Phone: (636) 549-8150
Linkedin.com/steven-denny-iba

ABOUT YOU DON'T KNOW WHAT YOU DON'T KNOW™

The phrase "You don't know what you don't know" is often used in our practice to describe an experience and process that many of our clients go through for the first time when we work together. It refers to a gap in knowledge that comes from lack of experience. We work with clients to make the experience as fruitful as possible.

My partner, Terry Lammers, and I decided to trademark this phrase and use it to write a series of books designed to share knowledge with business owners. Our vision is to write about things we know that are not well known—buying and selling businesses, valuing businesses, working with trusted advisers, etc. We hope our books will help fill that gap in knowledge.

This book is the second in a series which we expect will grow in number. Our publisher, Nancy Erickson of Stonebrook Publishing, has developed an incredibly useful process for us to write these books. If you have a book in you, we strongly encourage you to go to www.TheBookProfessor. com to learn more about how to get your idea on paper and into the marketplace.

We invite you to go to:

www.YoudDontKnowWhatYouDontKnow.com and register to find out more about our other products and offerings. As a registrant, you'll be able to review future books, download samples, and benefit from additional resources that are complementary to the book series. You can also connect with us and share your feedback.

We encourage you to share the book and resources with others in your circle of friends.